T0010640

# REWILD
# YOUR MIND

# REWILD YOUR MIND

## Use nature as your guide
## to a happier, healthier life

### NICK GOLDSMITH

WELBECK

Published in 2023 by Welbeck

An imprint of Welbeck Non-Fiction Limited
Part of the Welbeck Publishing Group
Offices in: London – 20 Mortimer Street, London W1T 3JW &
Sydney – 205 Commonwealth Street, Surry Hills 2010

www.welbeckpublishing.com

A CIP catalogue record for this book is available from the British Library.

ISBN 978-1-80279-391-8

Typeset by seagulls.net

Illustrations by Eliana Holder and Shutterstock

Printed in Great Britain by CPI Books, Chatham, Kent

10 9 8 7 6 5 4 3 2 1

To my boy Finn

May you always be able to find the same level of connection and sense of grounding in the present, that I have from spending time in the great outdoors.

No matter what you go on to face in life, know that the answers lay within and are never far from your grasp.

# Contents

# FOREWORD

Excuse my French, but Nick knows his s***. He knows about the great outdoors, and he also knows, based on his own personal experiences, how getting out into the wild can benefit your mental health and wellbeing. As someone who has been through mental health issues myself, and who has also spent a lot of time outdoors – in the military and on other adventures – I can tell you that this book is on point. It's raw, thought-provoking and inspirational. It's also wise and passionate.

On every page, you sense Nick's passion for spending time in the natural world and rewilding yourself. Reading this book is like spending time in Nick's company – he's always encouraging you to be in nature, and always has something to teach you. Nick and I are both former Royal Marine Commandos, and we met more than ten years ago in the jungles of Belize on exercise. I can't think of another former Marine who loves being in the wild as much as Nick does. For years, Nick has been keeping me informed about the new life he has built for himself in nature, which has been great to see. All his best stories, his deep knowledge and his insight are in these pages, which will teach you how to thrive in nature and, even more importantly, how to enhance your health and wellbeing.

## REWILD YOUR MIND

As Marines, we demonstrated a Commando spirit every day. That same spirit runs through this book from cover to cover – courage, determination, unselfishness and cheerfulness in the face of adversity. And always being able to find the silver lining in a situation. The great outdoors also teaches you that. This book is for anyone and everyone who wants to get back to nature, and to feel happier and healthier. And I think that must be all of us.

**Jason Fox**
*August 2022*

# INTRODUCTION

Nature saved my life. Nature stopped me from switching myself off.

That's not some hyperbolic first line to hijack your attention – it's the reality, as raw as it sounds. If I hadn't had a deep love and connection with nature, I wouldn't be here today. I would be a statistic – yet another burned-out Royal Marine Commando who survived daily contact with the enemy in Afghanistan but was unable to deal with the aftermath, with the coming home part. Psychologically, war had turned me inside out. I was fried. I had reached a point when I didn't care whether I lived or died, when I felt as though I might just switch myself off.

Nature pulled me back from the edge.

That, in essence, is why I've written this book. The fact that nature kept me alive is something I'll never forget, and which I reflect on most days. Now, I want to show *you* how to rewild yourself, because – whatever your story – it will make you happier, healthier and more at peace with the world.

This isn't intended to be a dark read. Rather, I hope you'll find it an inspiring, hopeful and practical book, and that my love and gratitude for nature will come through on every page.

I'm going to be encouraging you to go wild every day, as well as showing you how to forest bathe, sleep under the stars, forage for food and talk openly around a campfire, among other ways of rewilding yourself. I like to think that if you can master the outdoors, you can master yourself.

First, though, I need to share my story so you can understand why I found myself numb from top to toe, not caring whether I was here or not, and the only place that felt right for me was in the woods, immersed in the wild. By reading what happened to me, you might start to appreciate why I believe so strongly in the healing power of nature, and why I feel that, after so much darkness in my life, nature is the light.

## ACTIVE SERVICE

Four gnarly tours of Afghanistan, where staying alive was a daily struggle, left me broken and self-loathing, and facing a firefight of a different kind. I was diagnosed with complex Post Traumatic Stress Disorder. Complex because it was the result of layer upon layer of devastating, disturbing and life-changing experiences.

Every day on those tours, we fought up close with the enemy, running through cornfields and into compounds, sometimes with our bayonets fixed, and I was often the first man in. Clearing rooms in a compound, I was throwing in high-explosive grenades and using a gas-operated, belt-fed weapon system that was capable of firing 600 rounds per minute, and my heart would be hammering in my chest at more than 200 beats per minute.

Every day was dicey. Every day was kinetic. Every day we were tested psychologically as well as physically. In the broiling, hellish heat, with temperatures sometimes exceeding 50 degrees Celsius, we conducted 18-hour patrols, some of which were down the notorious, high-walled Pharmacy Road in Sangin, Helmand Province, where there was no way of escaping the enemy. We were on high alert for snipers, tripwires, booby traps and murder holes.

## Know your enemy

The enemy ranged from locals who had been given a fistful of dollars to toss a grenade or fire a few rounds at us, to hardened, foreign fighters. Some of them were clearly well-versed small arms tacticians who got us into some tricky situations. Finding yourself cut off or surrounded was commonplace. Discussions about saving the last round for yourself were also common, which gives you an idea of what we had to think about before stepping out the door each day.

In the movies, someone gets shot once and they go down – but that wasn't our experience. Our super-light 5.56mm rounds would often go straight through the enemy; they weren't designed for killing outright, but for mortally wounding and incapacitating in conventional warfare. It would then take two soldiers to remove the injured man from the battlefield. Yet, this was far from conventional warfare. If we needed to kill the enemy outright, we had to shoot them in the head, which was made all the harder by them zigzagging as they ran towards us (which was also how we moved when running towards them).

From our encounters in the bazaar, it was clear that our enemy weren't scared of us; fighting-age males would give us death-stares from their motorbikes and I just knew that we would see them again. They were fearless, perhaps emboldened by the drugs they were taking, which included heroin; they would pull the needles out of their arms, then run straight at us through the corn with their Kalashnikovs, more than happy to meet their maker. If you were captured, having your head cut off would have been a kindness – the preferred practice was for a medieval-style torture in which you were skinned alive and had salt rubbed into your body.

This was up-close, visceral fighting. I survived ambushes, temporarily lost my hearing from massive explosions, watched some of my colleagues get shot right in front of me, and, on many occasions, narrowly avoided losing my own life. Returning to base, you sometimes only had a couple of hours of sleep before getting ready to go out on the next patrol, so your brain hardly had a chance to begin processing what you had just experienced.

## Victims of war

Seven times in the space of six months, I carried a friend's coffin. And in the same six months, the bloodiest time of the conflict for British troops, I attended or had duties at a further seven funerals. At every one, my brain was saying to me, "It should be me in that box". One of our chaps was buried in the same church that he had been married in just seven weeks earlier. I watched families fall apart as the realisation hit hard that it was their husband, uncle, brother or son inside that box. I know that lessons have since been learned but, at the time, it was lads from the same unit, who had just been fighting on the same tour, who were carrying the coffins. I can't hear Mariah Carey's

"Hero" without imagining coffins going up in flames at a cremation; if that track ever comes on the radio when I'm driving, I turn it off straight away.

I witnessed civilians getting caught in the crossfire and encountered child combatants. One of the worst experiences was having to deal with a group of children who had been brought to our location after they had been gassed by enemy fighters for going to school – for wanting to learn how to read and write. Four were already dead in the back of the truck, while others were gasping like fish out of water, having been sprayed with a homemade concoction that had attacked their nervous systems. They filled all the remaining hospital beds where they were given CPR. I felt helpless. It was rough to witness. I also saw evidence of commonplace child abuse by foreign fighters. I remember a little kid who had been shot and was brought to our base in a wheelbarrow. Of course, the big question on everyone's lips was, "Christ, was it one of us who did that?" It was possible, as bullets would ricochet everywhere when we were fighting in a built-up area. Then we discovered that the child had been shot at nearly point-blank range by his own parents in order to get the compensation dollars that our military provided. Life was cheap out there, even cheaper in war.

## War wounds

As if my life wasn't complicated enough, I injured my knee on my first tour during a skirmish with the enemy. Jumping across an irrigation ditch, I fell to my knees, John Travolta-style, and landed on some tree roots. I was in so much pain that I could barely walk. I put on a brave face and finished the patrol, but on my return to base the medic told me I had to leave the battlefield, which was devastating. I was absolutely beside myself. I felt as though I had been wrenched from my family – my military family. For the first time in my life, I was getting stress-related acid reflux.

I would end up having two operations on my knee. I'm pretty sure that the guy who replaced me lost his life on that tour. That's something I have to carry with me. For a very long time, a large part of me believed it should have been me. There's still a part of me that believes that I should have died on that tour, but I try to move forward.

## Home discomforts

We would return from this unpopular war and sense that the British public didn't want to know us. We didn't feel wanted. Getting turned away from nightclub doors made us feel particularly unwelcome.

Despite being burnt out from the first tour, I still did three more. I was self-harming by training almost to the point of self-destruction. I would go up and down a rope for an hour while wearing a respirator mask, rage as I smashed the punchbag, and manically lift and do shuttle-runs with 50kg dumbbells. I couldn't ever switch off. I was completely overwhelming my central nervous system.

The only time I found some relief from the hyper-vigilance that active service required was on leave when I went for a night out. I used to call it "pulling pin", as you would on a grenade. I would go out and get blotto drunk. I would walk around nightclubs with two bottles of Champagne, one in each hand. As would other Marines, who were probably dealing with the same pain, though I never knew for sure as I didn't say a stinking word to anyone about what was going on in *my* head.

We called those 'millionaire weekends', as you would spend £500 on booze. As a young Marine, the peer pressure to drink was massive: you couldn't ever say no to a night out, even if it meant you would have nothing left in your bank account and would struggle to feed yourself for the rest of the month. Live fast, die young, as tomorrow you could be sent on an operation. As time went on, I didn't need an invitation to drink, and I didn't care that I was spending all my wages on booze or that I was drinking to excess. Death or running out of cash, I didn't care about either of those. My card was just a piece of plastic, it meant nothing to me. All I could think about was the guys who weren't there. I was telling myself to live big because they couldn't. I was physically doing myself in while mentally beating myself about the head. I longed to black out, just so the pain in my head would stop.

My behaviour spiralled badly after the first tour. Uncharacteristically, I found myself fighting, drinking more and more, and caring less and less. Until that point in my life, I had always been a disciplined individual, but that was now out of the window. If someone in a club wanted a fight, I didn't give a f*** and I would fight them. I now recognise I had the ability to become quite a scary character.

As soon as things started to hit hard at home, I would go into ops mode: short, sharp, cold and hard, and with little time for flowery speech or faffing about. It's something that seems to be common among veterans, emergency services workers and other high-performance individuals. It's a conditioned response, I guess. I wasn't a nice person when I was like that. I could be savage. Fearing that some undesirables, and possibly also the authorities, were looking for me after one late night/early morning booze-fuelled altercation, I ran 23 miles back home, most of it along a dual carriageway and the rest across muddy fields, despite having had a skinful of booze. I was a machine back then.

All the trauma had left me very angry – with everything and anything. If I was driving and someone cut me up at a roundabout, I'd get road rage, which I find hard to admit as I now crawl along the country lanes in the valley around my home.

To add to my psychological distress, my mother was battling grade 3 breast cancer and wasn't in a good place. She had had enough of the chemo and was at her wit's end. She needed my love and support.

Even when I was between tours, I seemingly couldn't avoid trauma. I had been drinking all day in my hometown and had been thrown out of a pub just before closing time. Looking for one final pint before going home, I found myself in a pub on the edge of town, and it turned into a lock-in. I passed out on the sofa, and woke to the sound of screaming. A girl threw a pint over me and shouted: "Do something!" I stumbled to the toilet where a local woman – someone I recognised from school – was bleeding out on the floor after a freak accident in which a shard of glass from the mirror had severed her femoral artery. Blood was spurting everywhere, all up the walls and as high as the ceiling. It was like a scene from a warzone, the place I was trying to get some respite from. In a moment, I went from blind drunk to sober. Fishing around in her leg for her artery, I got a face full of her blood.

For 19 minutes, the pressure from my thumbs was all that stopped Kirsty from dying. She lost half the blood in her body.

When the paramedics arrived and took over, I walked
the three miles home, stripped off by the back door,
and would later burn the clothes soaked through with
her blood. I was traumatised by the event. It's taken me
years, and lots of therapy, to realise that I saved a life. I'm
forever bonded with Kirsty, who has been such a warrior
and become a friend. After more than ten years and more
than 60 operations, including one to amputate her leg,
she is now happier than I have ever seen her. At the time,
the lesson I took from that bloody, horrific night was that
I would never be able to switch off, as I could be called
upon at any moment. No one else in the pub could have
dealt with that situation. No one else had my training or
had been conditioned by a brutal tour. That confirmed in
my head that I could never relax as things could go wrong
very quickly at any moment.

## Post Traumatic Stress Disorder

While that night in the pub would undoubtedly have been
a contributing factor, along with the massive facial trauma
I suffered while playing rugby for the Navy between tours
(breaking my eye-socket in three places as well as my
cheekbone and nose), my complex PTSD can mostly be
traced back to the war in Afghanistan. Consumed with
paranoia, shame and survivor's guilt, and fuelled by rage and
black coffee, I often didn't sleep. And when I did sleep, I was
having violent dreams that felt so vivid and real that I took
myself to see the psychiatric nurse. In one dream, I could
hear the enemy running through the cornfields towards me
and I couldn't find my weapon. I was reaching around in my
bed for it, panicking. That was during the tour on which I
was having multiple panic attacks every night.

I was finding it increasingly hard to tell what was real and
what wasn't. Two clandestine operations – which I can't

say much about – brought on acute paranoia surrounding personal security, to add to the hyper-vigilance I had already been experiencing. I put Blu Tack over the camera and microphone of my phone, so certain was I that I was being spied on by foreign intelligence agencies. Scared for my safety, I changed the front door to one without a letterbox, and installed a clear plastic box for our post to be dropped into – I would watch that box from the bay window, only approaching when I felt it was safe to do so. Just in case I had to suddenly disappear for a while, I kept a grab bag in my car, and to shake off my imagined "tail", I would drive round roundabouts twice and take diverted routes back to the house.

There's a picture of me at the end of my very last tour, and I clearly look unwell – I have the classic thousand-yard stare. I came back from that tour and I was just looking through people. But my superpower now is that I recognise others who are now in the same place I was then – and I have so much time for people in that place. I'm very gentle with them. No one is born that way. They're just responding to something that has happened to them or is happening to them right now.

## A WAY FORWARD

It doesn't matter whether you're a veteran or not, we all bleed, we're all human, and we've all been through something or are still going through something. Being in nature can only help you to turn things round.

I'm hoping this book will be a guide and companion to anyone looking to spend more time outdoors. Reconnecting with the wild can help to restore anyone's wellbeing and happiness.

When I say that nature saved my life, I should perhaps be more specific: it was buying a piece of wild woodland in the West Country that saved me. I know I'm fortunate to have my own woodland, but this book is not only for those living within easy reach of the countryside – it's just as much for those who live in the inner city, perhaps even on the top floor of a tower block. I believe anyone has the ability to rewild themselves – as long as they want to.

And this isn't an instruction manual on how to be super-macho or hardcore in the great outdoors – it's a guide to proven techniques that will enhance your relationship with the natural world and give you a greater sense of self-worth, purpose and identity, as well as confidence.

An entire generation of Marines and other service personnel have been damaged by the war in Afghanistan. The suffering caused one officer to be relieved of his command halfway through a tour, others ended up in the recovery centre or on strong anti-depressants. We have all looked for ways to deal with what happened. Tragically, some of the guys couldn't find a path, and took their own lives.

I'm self-aware enough to recognise that my story is a little different. Former Marines don't tend to study the ethnobotanical uses for trees, plants and flowers, or make YouTube videos about the delights of forest bathing (setting up a hammock between the trees, getting in and immersing yourself in nature and the moment). As far as I know, I'm the only former Marine who is working in nature from this angle.

## Returning to nature

I suppose I've always had an affinity for nature. People imagine that one of the reasons you join the Royal

Marines is because you had a chaotic childhood. I had a great childhood, most of which I spent outside. As a boy, nature was where I went to have fun and adventures with my friends. I suppose you could say I was raised as a "posh Redneck" in southern England, spending my days camping, fishing, playing rugby and ripping the skin off my knees.

As a Marine on tour, I didn't have the same connection with nature. Out on a patrol, I could hardly stop and admire the landscape or pick fruit from a tree. If I was looking at my natural surroundings, it was to find some cover from fire, or to locate a hedge where I could set up an OP (observation post).

Going back into the woods, I felt safe again. I reconnected with my childhood. Without the woodlands, I wouldn't have come through those bad times. Initially, it was somewhere to go, but over time it became much more than that. The woods gave me a new life, and a new identity, as I prepared for leaving the military and for when I actually left.

As a Marine Commando, you live in an elite world and you have to believe your own hype – that you're the biggest, baddest thing out there on the battlefield. You're part of a group of high-performance individuals who are working towards a common goal – the mission. You need a massive ego. But then when that's all over and you're no longer a Marine, you have to ask, "Who am I?" The woods helped me to answer that question. Working on my woodland, and building an off-grid wooden cabin, enabled me to put myself back together.

Away from the base, the barbed wire, the ID cards, the egos, and the version of myself that I had chosen to live

with for so many years, I could start to work out who I
was without a green beret on my head. Who was I free of
the corps, when I didn't have a uniform to wear, a place
to be and a time to be there? I could start to ask the real
questions in the woodlands.

## A slow recovery

Nature wasn't an instant healer. It was a slow process,
perhaps because my PTSD is complex. I wasn't an easy
fix. At first, I suppose, I was a crazy man in the woods.
There was the bitter, snowy night when I walked into the
woods on my own, lit a fire and stared into the flames,
before passing out from drinking too much rum. I still
didn't care whether I lived or died. I was still numb. I had
taken a bottle with me into the woods as that was the
fastest and most cost-effective way of switching off my
brain. It wasn't that I felt a strong command voice to end
my life, but I no longer cared if I lived or not. I woke up still
clutching the bottle, my body dusted with snow. My wife
Louise – who has been my rock, and a source of constant
love and support over the years – thought that I could
have died that night, alone in the woods. She had already
been through months of me sitting on my own in the dark
in the living room – there was no stimuli around me but
my head would be going at a hundred miles an hour.

That was my lowest point. But, slowly but surely, nature
helped me to care again, to want to live, to find myself.

The reason I had got so low and ended up in such a
wretched state was because I had somehow slipped
through the net. The armed forces had recognised
something wasn't right, diagnosed me with complex
PTSD and sent me on leave. While it was decided that
I should go into the Naval Recovery Service Centre,

in reality, no one made sure that happened and that I actually started my treatment. The truth is, they forgot about me.

That screw-up only made things worse. When Louise came home from work, she never knew what she would find and that scared her. I had been on leave for about eight months and was at my absolute lowest point when I finally reached out for help, contacting the only person I trusted: the psychiatric nurse who had dealt with me on my final tour. Within a week, I was in the Recovery Centre. If I had gone straight into therapy, I think I could have made a better, faster turnaround. Thankfully, I had nature to help me through.

My craving for a new identity came with a desperation for knowledge. I went on courses and read hundreds of books, adding to the bushcraft knowledge and survival skills that I had built up as a boy and as a Marine when deployed in the Middle East, the Arctic, the desert and the jungle. Every night in the recovery centre, I was carving spoons. The cleaner complained most mornings about the wood shavings scattered across the floor. While I did everything that was asked of me there – from hydrotherapy to acupuncture to cognitive behavioural therapy to eye-movement desensitisation and reprocessing (EMDR) – it was the woods that kept me alive. That was what kept me going every day.

I had internalised everything for years. It was only when I was in therapy that I started unpicking it all. The next part of the process was going into the woods and sitting around a campfire talking. In the woods, I found a safe place to open up to others about my experiences and the psychological damage I had suffered from going to war.

# A LIFE FOR LIVING

Rewilded and reenergised, I established Hidden Valley Bushcraft, a bushcraft business teaching others forest skills, and even created a woodland kindergarten. Together with Louise, a former detective constable, I have built a new life that is firmly rooted in the land. Most meaningful of all has been my Woodland Warrior Programme, in which I take military veterans and others into my woods for a weekend of outdoor activities and honest chats around the campfire. At the exact same spot where I once passed out in the snow, full of rum and self-disgust, I give them the space to discuss their own inner turmoil, including sometimes their own suicidal feelings as they come to terms with their experiences.

It's the soft skills, not the hard skills, that have taken me furthest since leaving the Marines. I no longer have to prove to myself that I know how to infiltrate a compound or how to kick someone's door down, or how to take someone prisoner – I've done all that. I'm now actively choosing to do something else with my life.

I was a hair's breadth from not making it. I allowed myself to become so ill that I didn't care about myself. And that is why I welcome people into my woods. I've helped a wide selection of people, including Helen, a former firearms officer for the Metropolitan Police who was suffering from PTSD after surviving being shot in the leg, being stabbed multiple times and the detonation of a bomb in a shopping centre.

I feel most alive when I'm outside in the elements. Where possible, I try to live a more natural life. Most days, I don't leave the valley where I live. While my experiences still plague me, I'm better at managing my complex PTSD.

I still don't like walking through cornfields as it triggers too many memories of Afghanistan. Louise will warn me if our boy, Finn, is using red paint at home, as that can be a trigger that takes me straight back to being in that pub toilet with Kirsty. I've had to reassess my relationship with alcohol. I used to be able to drink a bottle of wine and hold it pretty well; if I have a glass of wine now, I feel pretty squiffy.

Thanks to the healing power of nature and to being outside every day, I'm in a good place most of the time. Being a dad has helped, too. I often find myself thinking: "How will this affect the boy?" To help prove to myself that I can now deal with the memories of Afghanistan, I've repurposed military kit for my new life – an old grenade launcher ammunition box has made an ideal oven in the woods, and I have surrounded that with cob, the same building material the Afghans used along the infamous Pharmacy Road. A parachute provides some cover from the rain when sitting round the campfire. Inside my home, I use an old explosives box for storing kindling, while a recycled 105mm artillery shell – like those that used to come in dangerously close to our positions – is where I keep the tools for the wood burner.

While I embrace modern technology, I'm also doing what I can to help preserve ancient traditions and to revive the age-old connection between mankind and nature. Nature gave me my life back and now nature can help you too. If you read on and then get out there and try some of the skills and activities in this book, it is likely this will have a positive impact on your mental health. I urge you to give them a go.

# HOW THIS BOOK WORKS

I've split the book into three parts.

## Part One – Relax & Rejuvenate

This section focuses on the accessible outdoor activities that will help you to destress – such as forest bathing, wild swimming and going wild every day – as well as how bringing nature into your home will allow you to feel more relaxed and able to reengage with the modern world.

## Part Two – Rediscover

This section will give you the inspiration and practical tips to thrive outside in the wild, such as sleeping under the stars, making a wild cup of tea, looking after your knives and axes, and foraging for food (without poisoning yourself). These are skills that our ancestors would have used every day, and which we can all rediscover.

## Part Three – Reconnect

The final section is possibly the most important for readers who are suffering with mental health issues or feel burdened by their problems. I want to show you how the simple act of sitting around a campfire and talking can help you to reconnect with others and also with yourself.

I'm here to help you engage with nature again, to reset and recharge. To rewild yourself.

# PART ONE

## RELAX & REJUVENATE

In Part One, I'm going to encourage you to use nature to relax and rejuvenate. I'll be urging you to go wild every day, to take up forest bathing, to try wild swimming and to bring nature into your home.

If you're able to get outside and embrace nature, it will enhance both your physical and mental health. Studies have shown that spending more time in the wild helps to soothe and relax you, leaving you more at ease with the world.

Every time you go for a walk, forest bathe or go wild swimming, you'll feel lighter. You'll clear your mind and always feel better for it.

Being in nature will also lower your blood pressure and cortisol levels, and you'll be getting active, which enhances your cardiovascular system and general physical fitness. Even forest bathing, which in essence is about doing nothing, still involves walking to where you're sitting!

# 1

# FOREST BATHING

Time out in a hammock somewhere wild or sitting at the base of a tree has become an essential part of my daily routine. In Japan, this is almost an art form, known as *shinrin-yoku*, which roughly translates as "forest bathing". However, no water is involved, and you can keep your clothes on! Forest bathing involves completely immersing yourself in nature and in the moment.

## RESCUE REMEDY

Practising this daily allows me to manage my complex Post Traumatic Stress Disorder and to live a full life. The time I spend bathing in nature keeps me just the right side of needing to be heavily medicated – I get a natural high from the body's own feel-good hormones.

Lying back in the hammock, with my eyes closed and listening to the birdsong and the wind in the trees, it feels as though I'm floating. In the Marines, we used to talk about "go slow" when you took it easy for an afternoon, and forest bathing must be the ultimate "go slow" activity in a fast-moving world. While they have been doing this for years in Japan, forest bathing seems more necessary than ever before in the West, offering an escape from the pressures of modern life.

There are still days – particularly when I'm tired – when my mind takes me back to being ambushed while on patrol during my first tour of Afghanistan; the enemy had been lying in wait for us behind a wall. Every day since that ambush has been a blessing; but when the images and the sounds from that day crash through, I'll find myself expecting something else to happen, for there to be some fresh horror to contend with. I've learned that this is just an emotion that I need to ride out. But if I'm really struggling to get through it, I'll change my environment, go somewhere green.

Sleeping in the middle of an English forest, I've spent hours re-running moments and decisions I took in the white heat of Helmand Province, asking myself: "Was that the right thing to do?" You might find yourself entering a dream-like state and having conversations with people who are no longer here; I hear them saying, "It's OK, mate, it's OK." I've often thought about the moment when I was about to clear a room in a compound by throwing in a grenade, putting my weapon on fully automatic and drilling everyone inside. Fortunately, I wasn't wearing my ear defenders that day and I heard something and stopped – the room was full of women and children. If I had thrown that grenade, I would have had to live with those deaths for the rest of my life.

Forest bathing always ensures that my head will soon be in a different, better space. More often, though, forest bathing is preventative – it stops me from feeling like that in the first place. Everyone has their own individual problems and concerns, but the joy of forest bathing is universal; there isn't a more gorgeous way to destress and process.

It has been found that forest bathing lowers your heart rate and cortisol levels. Scientists from Japan, as well from other countries around the world, have researched the benefits of spending time in a forest, showing how it can lower cortisol levels, as well as your heart rate and blood pressure. The beauty of being in the forest – where you can enjoy the trees, the birdsong and the smells, and perhaps, if you're lucky, the dappled light – is that the non-threatening environment keeps you from going into fight-or-flight mode. Studies have shown that being in nature will soothe and calm you. For me, it is a safe place where I am comfortable pressing pause. Being in the hammock allows my brain to start working on things that it wouldn't otherwise get a chance to process. In the modern world, we're always stimulated and there's always something to think about; in nature, everything feels simple again, and that gives you the mental capacity to deal with other issues. Nature gives you the mental clarity and space to see the bigger picture, rather than getting bogged down in the nitty-gritty of your busy life. In a green, gorgeous forest, you can allow your brain to zone out.

Another benefit of forest bathing is that your body will be absorbing the organic compounds released by trees and plants. Known as phytoncides, they naturally boost your immune system and help your body to fight tumours and viruses. I'm fascinated by this, with research showing how being in nature enhances the production of killer T-cells, which are anti-cancerous.

# THE ART OF FOREST BATHING

Wherever you are in the world, forest bathing is the perfect way to log off from the modern digital age and reconnect with the natural world. Forest bathing allows you to forget all the stresses and confines of today's society. Lying in a hammock or on the forest floor, looking up at the tree canopy, you'll feel as though you're truly at one with the forest. You're just letting yourself be. You've got no agenda. Nothing to do. Nothing to chase. Nowhere else to be. Nothing else matters right now but kicking back and taking it easy in the forest.

You've taken the weight off your feet, and it really can feel as though you're relaxing in a bath. Allow your mind to wander wherever it needs to. If you've been through any trauma, your mind may want to bring that up sometimes. But don't worry as this is a safe place where you can take control of the situation. You can learn to push those feelings away and instead focus on something else, maybe a part of your life that is going well.

It doesn't matter if you live in a city and can't go into a forest every day, you can still forest bathe. Sitting at the base of a tree – which could be in a city park or wherever you find a small bit of green space – is also a form of forest bathing, which I've been doing since I was a teenager. Sit back, get comfortable and take the opportunity to use your senses to connect with the natural world around you.

I was a boy when I discovered the joys of sitting at the base of a tree. Most weekends, I would go into the woods with Chris, my best mate from childhood and still one of my closest friends. Some days, we would be there for hours, hardly moving and being as quiet as possible, watching the deer and other animals. The quieter we were, the more the animals would approach us, and we had some brilliant interactions with big stags. They were investigating a foreign scent in their woodland and they could see, from how still and quiet we were, that we weren't a threat to them. Those were the moments – up close with the stags – when we truly felt part of the woodland.

Having your back to a tree is so calming, and I think that's an evolutionary thing. We hairless chimps are poorly designed – our field of vision is very limited. When you're sitting at the base of a tree, you're protected from being attacked from behind; you don't have to worry so much about what's around and you can relax.

## LEAVE THE EVERYDAY BEHIND

Like anyone else, I come into the woods with the business of the modern world bouncing around my head. I'm thinking about the emails I need to reply to and everything else on my to-do list. Entering the woods, I may be walking faster than I need to, as I still feel the urgency of the modern world. If my steps are clumsy and I'm not noticing my surroundings as I usually would, those are signs that I need to spend some time forest bathing.

Within 20 minutes of climbing into a hammock or sitting at the base of a tree, I start to feel the benefits. I feel as though I have become part of that woodland, but not as a predator looking to harvest something from the landscape. I'm not there to control nature, as humans often wish to, but to be part of it. After a couple of hours of forest bathing – which is about the right amount of time for me – I will be completely relaxed and fully recalibrated. And I won't be worried about re-joining the world; I will be ready for it. Being in the forest is the most natural environment you can be in – after all, we humans evolved in the great outdoors.

You don't have to have had a diagnosis of something, or to be suffering from anxiety or depression, to benefit from forest bathing. I would encourage everyone to try it. You also don't have to do it for a set amount of time; half an hour two or three times a week, or even just once a month, is going to enhance your wellbeing. Remember that prevention is always better than cure. Lying in a hammock in the woods, lying on the forest floor, or sitting at the base of a tree in a city park is only going to help you feel calmer and happier.

## FREE YOUR MIND AND SENSES

Don't walk into the forest with an agenda. If you find that hard, calmly tell yourself: "I have nowhere else to be. I don't have anyone to answer to, and nothing else is important in this moment. I'm just going to be in the forest. I'm just going to allow myself to be." If you can keep giving yourself that message, you will start to believe it.

Sometimes I'll fall asleep. In the UK, that's generally perfectly fine, as nothing's going to come and peck my eyes out. But I would be slightly more cautious in, say, certain parts of the United States, as I wouldn't want to wake up to find myself being chewed by a mountain lion.

### Engage all your senses

Smell the forest. There's something calming about the smells in the wild. Those smells will change through the seasons, but they will always help you to feel more relaxed.

Appreciate how every wood or forest sounds different. The sound of the wind in the trees is comforting white noise. For me, it also cancels out my tinnitus, which I've had since an ambush in Afghanistan (for three days afterwards I couldn't hear anything apart from a ring with a solid tone). I like how every forest can often sound different, and also changes every day. For example, in a pine forest, it sounds as though you're by the sea, listening to the surf hit the shore. That's actually the sound of gusts of wind pushing past thousands of little needles. When you're in a broadleaf forest, you will hear the wind less and the native fauna more. I recall trips to the far north of Norway, where the forest was very, very quiet. Hundreds of miles inside the Arctic Circle, the Northern Lights made the night skies an incredible sight, but the forest was somehow always silent.

## HOW TO USE A HAMMOCK

### What you'll need

If you're going to invest in a hammock, I would recommend one with a small pocket to store your phone (switched off, of course). I also like to take off my watch and put that in the pocket, zip it up and forget about time. For the sake of the forest, use tree straps made out of seatbelt-like webbing, as they will help to prevent damage to the bark. You'll also need a couple of carabiners to attach the hammock to the webbing straps.

### Where to bathe

Ideally, find a spot that will activate your senses, such as close to a stream or a babbling brook, or somewhere that allows you to enjoy birdsong, a view, or the sound of the wind dispersing through thousands of pine needles. You'll need to find a couple of trees that are close together and strong enough to support you and your hammock.

## Setting up the hammock

As you're tying the straps around the trees, keep your hammock around your shoulders. This stops it dragging on the forest floor and getting wet, which would spoil your enjoyment when you get in. Always put the straps higher up the trees than you think you might need, so approximately five to six feet from the ground, as the hammock will sag when you get in, especially if you're on the heavier side, as I am. You want to ensure that there's a gap between the bottom of the hammock and the forest floor of at least a foot as otherwise you're going to feel cold and won't be able to relax. Putting a foam mat at the bottom of the hammock will also stop you from getting cold and give you extra comfort.

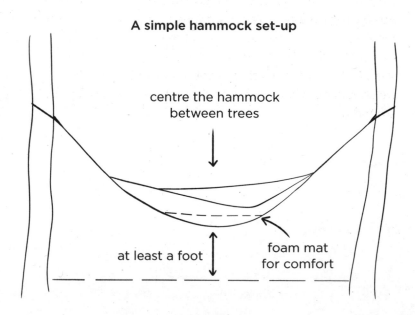

**A simple hammock set-up**

centre the hammock
between trees

at least a foot

foam mat
for comfort

## Getting into the hammock

Find the middle point of the hammock and sit down as
if you're getting into a chair. You'll know quite quickly if
one or both of the tree straps are not attached properly
and needs adjusting. Next, put one hand on each side and
swing your feet up and into the hammock, and lie down.
It's important that your feet are not higher than your
head, otherwise all the blood will go to your head.

If you have a larger hammock – you could even invest
in a double-sized one, as I have – you can pull the
material round you. I recommend doing that if you're in
an area where there might be midges, ticks or insects
that could disturb your peace – you want to be left
alone in your cocoon.

## Mix it up

Once you've found your ideal little spot, you'll inevitably
want to always go back there (we're creatures of habit).
But try to find a few places for forest bathing and rotate
them as if you always go back to the same place you'll
eventually damage the trees, even if you're using tree
straps. There's not much ancient woodland left, and
we should do what we can to protect the environment
around us.

# Breathing exercises

I've noticed that people breathe differently in front of their peers or when they are in the city than when they're in nature. When you're with people you're hoping to impress, you're trying to keep your form at all times. Back when I was an ego-driven, high-performing Marine, I was always trying to inflate my chest with my breathing, as I thought that was what alpha males were supposed to do. But breathing properly is about filling your lungs and allowing your stomach to move forwards and backwards. Being in nature, away from people, you instantly feel as though you can breathe more easily.

Once you're settled in your hammock, try the following breathing exercises.

## Calming breath

- Breathe in through your nose for five seconds, and exhale for five seconds.

- Breathe in through your mouth for seven seconds, and exhale for seven seconds.

- Think about each breath and count them in your head. You'll feel one of the body's natural feel-good drugs, being released.

- Really feel each breath, right to the top of your lungs.

- By about the third or fourth round of this breathing exercise, you should really feel a sense of calm.

**7–11 breathing**

- Breathe in through the nose for seven seconds and out through the mouth for 11 seconds.

- Make sure you breathe out slowly, in a controlled fashion and for longer than your in-breath – your body will then release its feel-good hormones.

- This exercise will give you the same feeling as when you give someone a hug, and it will help you to relax and destress.

When we came under fire in the Marines, we were taught to breathe in for four seconds and breathe out for four seconds. If you're being ambushed, when the first bullet comes in you need to have enough oxygen in your brain for the training to kick in and for you to do what you need to do. The breathing exercise was intended to avoid a big exhalation of breath when you have a sudden shock, because, a second later, if you haven't taken cover and returned fire, another bullet might come in and get you. That's why breathing was always so important in those moments. I've always known the power of breathing, and how it can change how you are feeling. Nowadays, lying in a hammock and breathing mindfully helps to soothe and relax my mind.

## REWILDING REMINDER

- Slow down, take it easy.

- As you recline in your hammock or sit back at the base of a tree, you're immersing yourself in nature.

- Forest bathing is your opportunity to take a break from the pressures of modern life and to connect with the natural world around you.

- You will feel calmer and happier for the experience, while also boosting your immune system.

# 2

# GO WILD
# EVERY DAY

Nature is the light. I think you only truly appreciate that when you've seen so much darkness. Just as each year has a summer, it also has a winter. You cannot fully appreciate one without having experienced the other.

I've experienced a level of horror that I'm hoping many of you couldn't possibly imagine. Only if you've been in a war zone or been a victim of war can you truly know what it's like to be choking on adrenaline, with terrible smells penetrating your nostrils, and the sound of gunfire and artillery making your ears throb and ring. I'm forever haunted by things I've seen, heard, smelt and done. Those images, sounds, smells and memories are still there – they don't go away, you have to find a way of managing them, which is where, for me, nature comes in.

Acute stress is relative to those who experience it. It can come about in many ways and at any time in our lives.

Remember we are all only human! If I ever went out into nature by choice as a Marine, it was to put a pack on my back and go for a long run. I would thrash myself up a mountain and back down again. Damaged, disturbed and in a horrendous mental state, I wanted to test myself against nature. As if Mother Nature was somehow the enemy, rather than the greatest friend I could possibly ever hope for.

Nature didn't feel like the light then. It just felt like somewhere else I would go to punish myself, fuelled by black coffee, rage and self-loathing. More darkness. I was forever pushing – training up to three times a day, always going to my physical and mental limits, or beyond and training to failure – I was chasing some kind of buzz. The worse the weather was, the more it felt as though I was taking on nature when I went for a punishing run across the landscape. I was either feeling nothing – there were times when I was so depressed that I could barely function mentally – or I was feeling too much. There was nothing in between. I look back at those times now and I realise that putting on a pack and beasting myself in nature was probably the last thing I should have been doing. I never gave nature the chance to heal and soothe.

It's only since leaving the military that I have come to see and feel that nature is the light. When I'm out in the wild today, I'm not thrashing myself – I either run to keep fit, or just go for a walk. Taking it slowly most days. Going at the pace that feels right, and that allows me to enjoy my surroundings and to feel the healing powers of Mother Nature.

I now recognise how important it is to go for a daily headspace walk, even if that's just for 15 minutes, as that's long enough to make a big difference to how I feel. Getting out, going for a daily walk and interacting with nature has a transformative effect on my mental state, and it's something that I encourage everyone to do every day. Being in nature, I'm so relaxed it's almost spiritual. I recently walked barefoot around a woodland, taking my boots off for a really lovely, grounding feeling (if you know your trees, you can avoid getting any thorns in your feet). It felt as though I was walking in my ancestors' footsteps.

You can walk into nature with a busy head – multiple thoughts, often loud, discordant and competing for attention – and leave with a quieter mind, with a sense you can handle the rest of the day. If you can embrace green space and take yourself away from the business of everyday life, you are giving yourself the chance to destress, clear your mind and improve your mental clarity.

## STEP OUTSIDE

Going wild doesn't necessarily mean being in ancient woodlands or somewhere very rural. Far from it. You don't have to be living in the countryside to get into the routine of going for a daily headspace walk in the outdoors.

Even if you live in the city, perhaps even on the top floor of a tower block, and you have to take the lift down 20 floors to get outside, there's more green space around you than you might have realised. Open your eyes and you'll see there are green spaces around, even if it's just pocket parks – small public spaces found in large towns and cities – which might only take a few seconds to walk around.

Most streets will also have trees. And, as I'll explain, going for a nature walk in the city is also about starting to notice what's around you, such as how the sun has bleached and changed the buildings around you. Think of them as mini, daily adventures in the wild.

Going wild every day, you'll start to engage with nature in a way you've never done before. You might even find yourself wanting to learn natural navigation (which, paradoxically, helps you to lose yourself in nature).

Maybe you're too comfortable being indoors. You may have become – sorry to have to tell you this – a sofa slug, not even leaving the house to get food as you can order dinner on an app and get it delivered to your door.

You might be questioning whether going wild every day – and getting out of your climate-controlled box for a few minutes a day – can really change how you feel and what's going on in your head. What's the point? So, consider that it's only very recently – just the blink of an eye really when you think about the history of human evolution – that we have been living inside boxes (houses). For the rest of our existence, approximately 300,000 years, we've essentially survived outside, in the elements. That is our natural habitat, not sitting in front of our widescreen TV, binge-watching Netflix.

If you really want to put this theory to the test, don't leave the house for two weeks and see how you feel. Ask yourself: if you are approximately 75% water, what happens to water when it stays still for too long? It stagnates and this is how you may feel. Follow this by going wild every day for the next fortnight. Feel the difference.

Hopefully you won't need to conduct such an extreme experiment to be persuaded that going for a daily walk is going to give you a mental boost, on top of all the additional physical benefits.

# HEALTH BENEFITS

In the depths of a British winter, when it gets dark by 4pm, a significant number of us will suffer from Seasonal Affective Disorder (SAD). The lack of natural light affects our mood, sleep and energy levels, and can potentially lead to depression. That's not something you can merely shrug off. I've had depression in the past, when every moment of every day was a fight to stay in the game. And I know that, if I don't look after myself, I could go back to feeling that way again.

With the shorter winter days, it can feel like a huge effort to get yourself outdoors, but it is the very time you need to get as much natural light as you can.

Being active and getting enough daylight plays an important role in our body's circadian rhythm, regulating when we're asleep and when we're awake during a 24-hour cycle. Our eyes, which act as the timepiece for our brains, aren't designed for artificial lighting, but for daylight and fire.

When you're outside, and your eyes are taking in natural light, your body will be awake and alert, ready to move and interact with the world. Being outside also tops up our supplies of Vitamin D, which has been proven to be key for the production of serotonin – sometimes known as the happiness hormone.

Psychologically, it's hard when you're getting up in the dark and coming home from work in the dark, but if you have a lunch break could that be the time to step outside and go wild for 15 minutes? And if you're really struggling with SAD during the darkest months, please speak out and tell your doctor. Or, if you find it easier, talk to a trusted friend and open up.

With mental health, the first hurdle to overcome is often being able to have an honest conversation with a friend. If you have someone in your life who you trust and can open up to, and who will tell you when you need help, I suggest you keep them close. The truth is, you're only ever going to have a handful of real friends in this world. What makes them true friends, I believe, is that you trust their version of reality and they trust yours. If you're not feeling right, you can start to question your version of reality. You no longer know which way is up. That's when you need a real friend. I am lucky enough to have a couple in Chris and Sledge, who keep me straight. They'll tell me if I don't sound right – maybe I'm getting worked up about something insignificant – and I'll always take note.

Whatever the time of the year, if you can get out there every day – into nature and into light – you'll feel so much better for it. I can assure you of this: no-one ever went for a headspace walk outside and came back feeling worse, and that's true even if it's pouring with rain.

When I was diagnosed with complex Post Traumatic Stress Disorder, I felt as though it was a horrible label to have to deal with. Over time, I have come to respect that diagnosis, and recognise I must look after my mental and physical health as otherwise I'm going to be in trouble. Going wild every day is an integral part of looking after myself. There's a specific place I like to go to every day. Find somewhere *you* love, or a route that you like walking, and which makes you feel good. Then make that happen every day.

# HOW TO APPROACH GOING WILD

Purposefully getting outdoors and into nature will very quickly result in your stress levels dropping and your mental clarity improving. Even the most reluctant person will quickly realise the outdoors isn't such a bad place after all.

## Find the time

Are you thinking you're too busy to even spare 15 minutes a day to go wild? Time is money, I hear you say. But what about time well spent? We're all busy, but everyone has time to go wild every day – everyone *needs* to have the time for some self-care.

Once you have been for a few walks, and are starting to feel better, you will no doubt make it a priority. Fifteen minutes is the minimum you should spend going for walk; if you can go for longer, even an hour or more, that's going to be even more beneficial.

## Find a reason to be out there

At first, you might need a reason to get outside, a motive for leaving the comfort of your four walls. That could be just walking around the block to see what's new in your area, or it could be going to the local shop to buy a newspaper. When I was starting my recovery, I was advised to get a dog as they said that would give me a reason to leave the house on those days when I didn't feel like it. So, I got Tilly, my fox red Labrador, who has been through so much with me, and who has been such an important part of my story.

But dog or no dog, once you start regularly getting outside, before long you won't need a reason to do so –

you will be choosing to be in nature as you can feel the benefits and want to keep caring for yourself.

## Go on your own or with a friend

If you want to be alone with your thoughts, or to work on an issue (be it work-related or personal) that's been eating away at you, then the outdoors might be the perfect place, particularly if your home is hectic.

On your own, you'll also notice more of your surroundings, keeping you grounded and present in the here and now.

Other times, you may feel like having company. Walking alongside a good friend provides a great opportunity for conversation. Friends can help you address any problems in a fresh way, and you could see movement on a sticky subject, helping you to take on a new perspective. By the end of the walk, you'll hopefully feel completely different about something that has been troubling you.

## Plot a route

If you're in a city, you will still be able to find at least three green spaces or slices of nature near you, and probably many more, it's just that you might not have noticed them until now. Plot a route that takes in all three, and which you can do every day. The beauty of having a regular route is that, with the changing seasons, you will start to notice more and more about the green spaces around you. Right now, you might be oblivious to the seasons, and how the trees and plants change through the year. After a few months of your daily wild adventure, without realising it, you will have become attuned to nature.

## WHATEVER THE WEATHER

Don't let rain, or even a storm, stop you going wild. They say the British are always talking about the weather, but that's not a problem. The problem is that we're forever *demonising* the weather. We look out of the window at a little light rain and immediately say, "Oh, bad weather today," and give ourselves a reason not to get outside. Too many of us in Britain are somehow only capable of leaving the house when it's a warm, still day, and we seemingly can't cope when there's rain, wind or snow, or if it's a cool day.

Transforming how you feel about the outdoors could start with changing how you talk about the weather, so consider the language you use. I'm also guilty of this – I'll sometimes catch myself talking about "bad weather". I'll tell myself that what I should be saying is simply, "It's raining. OK. So I'll put a coat on." There, problem solved.

Like most outdoorsy people, I believe there's no such thing as bad weather, just bad clothing. If you're going to invest in anything after reading this book, buy a waterproof coat. It doesn't have to be expensive, and it will enable you walk in any weather, and you won't care if it's raining. It removes the excuses. There's now no reason why you can't get out there each and every day and interact with nature. If you're a parent, changing how you speak about the weather will set a good example for your children, as you don't want them to think you only go outside when the sky is blue.

Getting caught in a storm, sheltering under a tree and waiting for it to pass, can be an exhilarating experience (just so long as it's not an electrical storm). Listen to the sound of the rain hitting the ground and falling through the canopy, and know the tree is protecting you and keeping you dry. That's a primal, lovely feeling, heightened by the heavily oxygenated air you get in a storm, with the rain pushing the oxygen down.

Being able to identify a tree that will protect you from a storm can give a small thrill – you're learning about nature, showing yourself that you can survive in the outdoors, even if you're still in a city park close to your flat. These are the moments that will boost your self-worth as you realise you're more resilient than you had imagined. You can problem solve and cope in the outdoors – you don't need to be confined to the indoors and the digital world.

There's another benefit to knowing which tree to shelter under in a storm – that knowledge helped me to impress Louise when we had just started seeing each other.

## DISENGAGE AND ENGAGE

### Digital break

If you're going to engage with nature, you'll need to disengage from the digital world. The best way to kickstart this is with your mobile phone. The best reason for using your phone when out and about in nature is to take photographs – looking around you for something photogenic can be a good way to engage with nature. Otherwise, keep your phone in your pocket or bag. This is a chance to stop scrolling through social media and to be absorbed by something more meaningful, the wild. By ignoring your phone, you allow your mind to go where it needs to.

Throughout the day, our brains are constantly trying to reset themselves, with lots of little reboots, and we all too often fill those moments by looking at our phones and giving our brains even more information, which actually *stops* our brains from rebooting. We're over-stimulated, and our mental health suffers as a result. So give your brain what it needs and step out of the digital world for a while. Use your walk as a digital break.

## Sensory checklist

When you're somewhere green, ask yourself what you can:

- see

- smell

- hear

- feel

- taste

If you're feeling stressed, going through that checklist will keep you in the here and now, stop you from fretting about what happened last week, and what might happen tomorrow. It will keep you in the moment. Running through your senses enables you to engage and interact with the world around you a little more each time.

Teenagers often walk around without two of their senses – they've got their hoods up, so they've lost their peripheral vision, and they're listening to music through their airpods so they can't hear what's going on around them. Don't do that!

Listen out for natural sounds, such as birdsong. Can you hear birds chirping? Even if you're in a busy city, surrounded by cars and people, you might be able to hear the birdsong, or even just the wind in the trees, when you walk through a small park. Birds often don't want to expend too much energy, especially during the winter months, so they won't move much, but that's when you can have some of the best interactions with birds.

## Be still

The ability to be still in the outdoors, and to become part of nature, will impact hugely on your mental state.

If you can be an observer, and take in everything that's happening around you without causing a disturbance, you're likely to have a calmer state of mind. Body and mind are linked, after all.

As a Marine, I would have to sit still for hours if I was in an observation post. Something as simple as scratching your nose could take 20 minutes, as you would have to move very slowly. You didn't know if a sniper had his crosshairs on you and if he was deciding whether to drop the hammer or not. If he was trying to work out who you were, and whether you were an enemy or not, any excess movement could have given you away. That ability to keep still for long periods is still useful in my new life.

# GET THE KNOWLEDGE

## Learn to identify trees and find water

When you get to each green space, do you know the names of the trees that are growing there? Could you also identity the flora and fauna? If you're not sure, it's okay to quickly get your phone out to take a photo, and to then research the tree or plant when you get home, but don't use this as an excuse to start looking at your emails.

If you're in the countryside, try to find your nearest water source on your walk. If you can see poplar, willow, alder trees or sedges, which are grass-like plants, that's a strong indication that there's water nearby.

If you find a babbling book or stream, sit and listen for a while, and you will soon feel quietly reassured. We're hardwired to want to discover water. That's because you will likely die if you don't drink water for three days. Water is life and water is security.

## Become a nature detective

By going on headspace walks, you will gradually condition yourself to the outdoors. Maybe without even realising it, you will become more at ease outdoors. Soon enough, you'll be ready to become a nature detective.

Whether you're walking in woodland, by a river or in a city park, it can be fun to look at the tracks on the ground and to try to work out who has been there earlier today or even yesterday. You can sometimes pick up information from the morning dew on the grass. If there is obvious disturbance of the dewy grass, that could be because a human or animal has passed through recently.

If you think it was someone walking their dog, try to find out more by asking questions such as these:

- How big was the dog?

- Was the dog walking or running?

- Can you tell whether it was a man or woman walking their dog?

- Can you guess how big the dog and humans were?

- Were the humans wearing trainers or wellies, etc?

- Which direction were they walking in?

If you're by water, can you see any frogs or fish, or paw prints in the mud or sand from voles, rats, otters or even larger mammals such as deer?

In the city or the country, are there any birds around? Where are they nesting? Can you see any nests or bird boxes? Walking in the woods near my house, I often notice a pile of feathers, which tells me that a bird was either pounced on by a fox or a smaller bird has been struck by a bird of prey; I can tell which by looking at the pattern of the feathers that have been left in. A bird of prey tends to create a large-diameter 'fairy ring' of the fine secondary feathers of its prey as a result of plucking, whereas a fox shakes its prey left to right and you are left with a liner scattering of feathers. A bird of prey will also 'surgically' pluck, leaving marks at the end of the feather, whereas a fox tends to leave the ends of the feathers chewed and covered in saliva.

If you can get into the habit of looking around as you walk, you'll start to spot more and more clues to the wildlife that exists alongside you. Keep asking yourself questions about your surroundings, as that will keep you in the present.

## WHAT MESSAGE ARE YOU TELLING YOURSELF?

One of the best things you can do is positive self-talk. When you get back from your headspace walk, make sure you tell yourself how much better you are feeling. You could also share that positive message with others, and encourage them to get out there as well. But your focus should always be on the message you're telling yourself, as that's what's going to help you to build yourself up. Whether you're saying it out loud or in your head, the message you tell yourself has real power over you.

If you're negative about yourself and your experiences, that has the potential to rip you apart. Other people in this world may judge you and make harsh comments, but you don't have to believe what they're saying. I'm speaking from experience when I say, if you're struggling and stressed and keep speaking negatively about yourself, those words and phrases will have a massive effect on you.

Instead, go for a walk, tell yourself you enjoyed it and try to disarm the negativity in your head.

# Natural navigation

One of the best ways of engaging with the outdoors, while becoming more self-reliant and less of a slave to your phone, is natural navigation – learning how to get about without a phone, map or compass, just as your ancestors did. This isn't some dark art, but a skill anyone can pick up if they just give it a try.

Natural navigation requires an active mind and calls on you to gather an understanding of the bigger picture and your immediate surroundings.

Navigation skills kept us alive in the Marines. On patrol in Afghanistan, we always had to know exactly where we were. While we had GPS, I was always making a mental note of where we were as you couldn't be completely reliant on the technology. Were we heading into enemy territory? If we had called in the artillery, it was imperative that we knew our position, otherwise you might be ordering shells to be dropped on your head. And if ambushed by the enemy, could I find my way back to base using only natural navigation?

In one clandestine operation in Africa, I was wary that my local driver, who ferried me to and from meetings, could betray me and deliver me to the local militia. The fear was having my head removed and ending up in bits in a suitcase. If I thought for a moment that my driver was going to give me up, I would need to jump from the car and find my way back to my hotel in the city. I would always concentrate on the direction I was heading in and for how long and made mental notes. I planned the journey in reverse, and created a story about the route that would help me to remember it.

At the same time, I built a rapport with my driver so he wouldn't sell me to the enemy and would warn me if some "bad men" (as relayed by him) had come to snatch me. And that's exactly what he did one day when I was in the bazaar buying some electronics. He was parked up nearby and called me, frantically saying that some men had spotted me go in and seemed to be looking for me. My driver might well have saved me from being snatched that day. That indicated I could trust him, but didn't stop me, as we drove through the city, from looking out for any landmarks that would enable me to find my way back.

While natural navigation is exhausting in potential life-or-death situations, it can actually have a positive mental effect on you when you're going for a headspace stroll.

## How to determine north, south, east and west

### Use the sun

On your daily walks, start to notice what the sun is doing, and where it is in the sky at certain times of the day (though that will change slightly at different times of the year).

If it's not overcast, remember that the sun rises in the east and sets in the west, so take your bearings from that.

On cloudy days, you need to look for where the sun has been. The northern side of a building won't get much sun, and will tend to go green, mouldy and mossy. Whereas the south side, which gets all the sun, won't be green. The sun might even bleach the south side of a building and cause the paint to crack off. Look at natural vegetation around you, which will lean towards the light, towards the south.

## Use the wind

In Britain, the wind tends to come from the south-west, though on a particularly bitter day there's a good chance it's coming from the north. It's a little harder in the city to use wind for navigation, because large buildings can block and divert the flow of air. But it's still worth thinking about the wind as it helps to build up a bigger picture in your head of the points of the compass.

## Use manmade installations

In a city, you can look up at the satellite dishes; in my part of Britain they tend to point south-south-east, but this may vary depending on where you are in the country, so do your research.

Religious buildings can also be helpful. Most Christian churches face eastwards, while most mosques in Britain face south-east.

## How to naturally navigate

This is a good mindfulness exercise as it keeps you in the moment. It's also great for building on your understanding of an area. And if you're a parent, it can be a fun activity to do with your kids.

- When you head out of the door, make sure you know the direction you're walking in – north, south, east or west.

- Be aware of how long you walk in that direction for.

- Every time you change direction, make a mental note, including how many minutes you walk that way for.

- Keep asking yourself, "Where am I? And where am I walking now?"

- Make a mental note of the natural landmarks and geographical features that you pass.

- When you get back home, find some paper and a pencil and see if you can draw a map of the route you've just taken. Add in the landmarks and features that caught your eye.

## REWILD YOUR MIND

This is stuff that I've done since I was a kid; but it was never so important as when I was recovering from the trauma I had experienced as a Marine. The observation and focus needed for natural navigation helped me to be more in the present, observing what was around me in the moment, rather than being caught in the past.

Once you start to get the hang of it, set yourself little challenges. Deviate from your usual route. Tell yourself to, say, walk north for five minutes and then turn east for two minutes, and so on. See where you end up, and then find your way back home.

These are lifetime skills that can be used all over the world. Once, years after leaving the Marines, while on an adventure in Lesotho, I found myself alone under a harsh African sun, at altitude and running low on water. I managed to navigate without a map or compass, and there's a quiet confidence that comes from that. And today, on rare trips to London, I like to walk to my meetings using natural navigation, telling myself a story as I go, so I know how to get back to my hotel.

**REWILDING REMINDER**

- Getting out into nature every day, even for just 15 minutes, will change how you feel and what's going on inside your head.

- If you're able to do that, whatever the weather, you'll feel all the better for it – you will discover for yourself that nature is the light.

- Be kind to yourself today and all days. Talk to yourself, listen to yourself, get to know yourself – this, combined with your engagement in the natural world, is the essence of rewilding.

# 3

# BRING NATURE INTO YOUR HOME

Your interaction with nature should always be as light as possible. Where possible, aim to leave no trace. Strictly speaking, the only thing you should take in the wild is a photograph, and the only thing you should leave is a footprint. But I think it's OK to pick up certain objects – twigs, pebbles, pinecones – when you're walking in a wood or along a beach or riverbank as that will let you bring nature into your home. Then, even when you're inside, you will feel a connection with the wild.

From burning those twigs after work on a Friday night, to keeping a smooth pebble in your pocket, to watching the pinecone react to what the weather is doing, there are some quick and easy ways to build that connection while helping you feel calmer and more relaxed at home.

# BURNING TWIGS

You might like to get into the habit of collecting twigs throughout the working week – a small handful each day, scooped up from the ground (and never broken off a tree). I encourage you to think of those twigs as representing your stresses of the week, and to make a pile somewhere in your home. On a Friday night, you can have the ritual of lighting a fire and throwing the twigs on. Watching them burn, it will feel as though your stresses are disappearing and you can relax into the weekend.

If you're going through a hard time right now, or there are some thoughts ruminating in your mind that you can't get rid of, write them down on a piece of paper, and cast that into the fire. Torching those words will help you to feel better and allow you to move on. Yesterday is the past. You can't change yesterday, but you can learn to let go of a problem in the past. If you are able to stay in the present, you'll get so much more out of today.

I don't want you to think I'm a pyromaniac, but I absolutely love the smell of fire. I talk about the importance of fire later in the book, but for now let me say how the smell of the smoke, as you burn your twigs and paper, is key to relaxing and soothing you. A smell can be powerful and evocative, and can sometimes change how you feel more than any other sense. I believe the smell of smoke is as beneficial for you as listening to your favourite song or eating your favourite food.

If you have a fireplace in your home, or space outside to safely have a fire, you might also like to gather firewood and sort it by size, as that can also be very therapeutic.

If you live in a flat, or anywhere without a garden or outside space, you won't be able to have a fire in your home, so maybe light a candle instead. Light that candle at the same time every day so it becomes part of your routine. Make yourself a cup of coffee or tea, sit down and while that candle is burning, stare into the flame. Enjoy that moment each day. An alternative would be lighting a joss stick, which I did a lot of when I was in the recovery centre. I chose natural smells, such as lavender, and found that helped me to feel a little calmer and reassured.

## PEBBLE IN YOUR POCKET

Ever since I burned out, I've carried a smooth pebble in my pocket as I find that enormously grounding. When I'm talking about something difficult, I play with the pebble with my fingers to help me to deal with the conversation. It's usually perfectly round or kidney bean-shaped, and it's wonderfully tactile, smoothed over hundreds of years by water, maybe rolled around on a beach somewhere. The pebble has seen many skies and sunsets and now it's in my hand, helping to keep my mindset rock-steady, and helping me deliver what I want to say. Whether I'm at home or away, on a busy train or outside in nature, I play with the pebble. Having busy hands is a way of keeping your mind quiet and calm.

Why I find the feel of my pebble so grounding dates back to times when man would have been knocking stones together every day. We're programmed to want to pick up pebbles, rocks and stones, and to feel them in our hands. While I've had a pebble in my pocket for years, it hasn't always been the same one. Pebbles come and go in my life, and that's fine by me. I have a pebble, I lose it and then I pick up a new one. Choosing a new pebble is part of the joy, as there's a story behind each one. You mustn't become too attached to any pebble because when you lose it – which you will – you will be distraught and might feel you can't go out into the world without it. I have also given my pebble to others who need it more than me. This simple act carries more power than you think.

# NATURE'S BAROMETER

As a little boy, we had gigantic pinecones – as big as my adult fist today – in our house. My mother had collected them from the French Alps, and placed one just inside the back door and the other outside on a garden table near the washing line. I would watch them in awe as they reacted to the changing weather. My childhood fascination hasn't dimmed. A pinecone is better at forecasting the weather than you or I could ever be by assessing atmospheric conditions, such as humidity. Its survival depends on predicting the weather as it's looking to spread its seeds. Years after being shed from the tree, a pinecone will still forecast the weather. It's smarter than you think and makes a lovely natural outdoor barometer.

### How to tell the weather from a pinecone

- Fully closed: it's raining, or there's rain coming

- Fully open: it's sunny, with more good weather to come

- Closed at the top, open at the bottom: rain possible, but not guaranteed.

Having a pinecone or two by your back door or on a window sill is a positive way to interact with the outdoors.

Why don't you pick up a pinecone in the park or wood and when you get home put it somewhere you can easily observe it every day? If you share my wonder of the pinecone, you will start to look at it to see what the weather is doing. If the pinecone is wide open, you might decide that today's a day to hang the washing out.

## CARE FOR A BONSAI TREE OR PLANT

In the chapter on forest bathing, I mentioned phytoncides, the organic compounds released by trees and plants, and how they can boost your immune system. The best way of exposing yourself to phytoncides is to be outside in nature, but having house plants in your home – or even a bonsai tree – can have a small but tangible effect on your body.

Whether it's a yucca plant, a spider plant, a bonsai tree or potted herbs, you will be required to water, prune and keep it/them alive, strengthening your bond with nature. Take a moment each day to interact with whatever you have brought into your home; maybe it needs more water or to be pruned. Try to do that at the same time every day, which will help you to create positive habits. It only has to be a few minutes a day, but it's time for you and your plant, and can be enormously beneficial. Find that space in your day.

## DISPLAY A PHOTO OF YOURSELF
## IN THE WILD

Climb a mountain, or walk a stretch of coastal path or long-distance trail. Experience a little bit of hardship – perhaps a few sore muscles – along the way, but also enjoy some beautiful views and a sense of achievement. Make sure you take a photo of yourself, which you can print and put somewhere prominent, such as on your fridge. If you're having a bad day, you can look at the picture and remind yourself how amazing you felt out there in the wild, and how you could be planning your next trip. If you don't feel physically up to something like this, go to the beach and listen to the sound of the crashing waves or visit a forest and bathe under the canopy, but remember to take a photo.

I've got photos of nature in the house. If I go somewhere beautiful and wild, I might take a picture and print it. It's about capturing the memory of that day so I can relive it when I'm at home.

# FISH

Somehow, I convinced my wife to get a fish tank in our old house, which I positioned at one end of the sofa. I would lie there after a busy day at work, watching the brightly coloured shapes moving about, and it was very therapeutic.

It's wonderful to watch as you're noticing how the fish aren't rushed or bothered; everything is slow. If you have a busy mind, it can help to fix your eyes on something that's moving slowly as your brain then starts to slow down and unwind. I think what I'm saying to you is this: be more fish.

## REWILDING REMINDER

- Even when you're back inside your home, you can continue building a deeper connection with nature, including with pebbles or pinecones or by burning candles.

- These natural aids will allow you to feel calmer and more relaxed.

- Be more fish.

# 4

# WILD SWIMMING

You emerge from the cold, wild water and you're so euphoric you feel lightheaded. Sunlight could be edging and dancing through the trees or you could be pulling yourself up a riverbank in the sheeting rain. It doesn't matter; nothing's going to bring you down from that natural high.

Maybe more than anything else you do in the outdoors, wild swimming – be it in a river, lake or the sea – makes you feel alive. You certainly don't get that same buzz from doing 50 lengths of backstroke in a heated, chlorinated, indoor pool under artificial lights. Colder than a pool, especially in winter, you will experience an initial shock, which instantly gets your body firing. While boosting your immune system, going for a wild swim is also going to raise your heart rate and metabolism while burning fat. Blood rushes to the surface of your skin.

But the most powerful transformation is not physical but mental, psychological and emotional. Your brain's flooded with endorphins, or happy chemicals, and you feel incredible. Free, exhilarated, energised. Lighter somehow. If you were feeling low or heavy before getting in, you'll feel completely alert on getting out; even just a few minutes in that refreshing wild water can change your mood, with studies showing it can help you to feel happier and to have a more positive outlook on life. For the full chemical effect, put your head completely under the water, even if it's just for a moment.

Any activity that makes you feel closer to nature is a good thing, and with wild swimming, you're not just close to nature but completely immersed in it. The thrill of wild swimming isn't just being in and under the cold water ,but also soaking in your surroundings. Pick somewhere wild and beautiful for your swim, and you'll get more out of the experience. And if you have to walk through countryside or along the coast to reach the water, then you'll be benefitting from a stroll in nature as well as a dip.

## WILD SWIMMING AND ME

Long before wild swimming became fashionable, I would swim in the river as a boy, playing around in the water with friends. I've always enjoyed the buzz of being in cold water, which is fortunate as becoming conditioned to it was an integral part of my training as a Marine. I once conducted cold water drills while part of an indigenous mentoring programme in the mountains of Afghanistan, where there was snow on the ground and I had to smash the ice with my fists before jumping in and submerging yourself. The more we were exposed and conditioned to cold water, the less chance there was of flinching on first hitting the water. That's what set us apart as Royal Marines – we were so conditioned to discomfort that we could operate anywhere.

I don't imagine many Marines would admit this to you, but it would be hard to find a more water-adverse bunch than those who have come through training and earned their green beret. As a group, when we have a choice, we don't tend to fancy getting wet. That's not because the thought of getting into icy water unnerves us, just that we tend to feel as though we've experienced enough of that already during the longest basic training in the western hemisphere: some 32 weeks!

Since leaving the military, I've felt myself drawn back to the wild water, as I know how it can lift my mood. In the Marines, being in wild water was all about hardening yourself up for fighting in all conditions, but now I'm no longer a soldier (I'm forever a warrior), it's about wanting to ride that wave of euphoria again. I look for a calm stretch of river, somewhere I can listen to the sound of the birds and where I might have the excitement of spotting a kingfisher.

While some wild swimmers are out all year round, even in the depths of winter, it's OK if you're like me and prefer to only go when it's a bit warmer. Go whenever you feel as though you will get the most from the experience – when you will get a natural high that you can take with you into the rest of your day.

If I know the thrill of going wild swimming, I'm also conscious of the dangers. While I don't want to put you off getting into the wild water, I think you should be aware of the potential risks involved. I'll never forget the time during Commando training when, dressed in our fatigues, we had to jump into Poole Harbour on a chilly December day and swim over to a capsized rib, right it and get in. We messed up the drill and ended up being in the water for far longer than we had imagined, around 10 or 12 minutes, which felt like an eternity.

The consequent temporary impairment was horrendous. When you're suffering with hypothermia, the mental impairment can be so severe that you become confused and disoriented and you don't even know where you are and what you are doing. That can be terrifying to go through. Everything slowed down for me, to the point at which I could no longer even figure out how the buckle on my bag worked. Putting one part of the buckle into the other should be the simplest of tasks, but it was beyond me. Another Commando recruit was curled up in the corner, crying. It was awful to see, but I think everyone who did that exercise was at the absolute limits of what they could tolerate. I got into the showers to slowly reheat, starting that painful process of the blood returning to your hands.

While I encourage you to go wild swimming, I encourage you to do so safely. I'm happy to share some breathing techniques, based on my training in the Marines and perfected since leaving the military, to cope with the shock of cold water. (Aside from the breathing techniques, the only other instruction before getting in cold water during Commando training was to "stop being so f***ing weak". As we were often told: "You're either here to get your green beret or you can f*** off.")

# BREATHING TECHNIQUES

Before you go wild swimming for the first time, get comfortable with being uncomfortable. Slowly introduce yourself to being in cold water. Start by having a shower at a regular temperature and then, at the end, switch to cold water. Over time, you can gradually increase the amount of time that you're under that cold water. To cope with a cold shower, you're going to need to practise breathing techniques that you can take with you into the wild.

- Breathe in through your nose for seven seconds, and then breathe out slowly through the mouth for as long as you can.

- Purse your lips, and make sure you're in full control of your breathing.

- Do as many cycles as you can, soothing and relaxing your body.

When you immerse your body in cold water, it will want to go into fight-or-flight mode, which can make you panic, your mind can shut down and you won't breathe properly. By focusing on your breathing, you're able to override that and take control of your body's response to cold water. Breathe through the shock of the cold water, try to normalise it. You're exposing yourself to the water, building yourself up. It can bring on a feeling of euphoria and put you in a positive state. If you can get yourself to the positive state then you're ready to make the move from the shower to the wild water.

# Wild swimming advice

### Never go alone

Wild swimming shouldn't ever be a solo activity. While some activities in nature – such as forest bathing – are best done alone in order for you to relax and fully engage with your surroundings, I would always urge you to swim with at least one other person. Even if you think you're a strong swimmer, always go with a friend, and ideally someone who has some experience of wild swimming. When many people get into cold water for the first time, their body will experience extreme shock and they can't help but let out a big gasp, with all the air rushing from their lungs. That's a dangerous moment as if your lungs don't re-inflate, you're at risk of drowning. There's this myth that when you get into trouble in cold water it's because of hypothermia, when the temperature of your body drops, but it's usually because of – the initial shock and the risk that comes from that involuntary gasp. Just so you're aware, if you're not used to being in cold water, there's also a small chance of a heart attack, though I should stress that's very rare.

Even strong swimmers, who could probably do lengths for hours in an indoor pool, can quickly get into difficulties in cold water. Whenever you go wild swimming, you need a buddy to look out for you. That goes both ways – you need to look out for your friend and check they're OK.

Beyond the safety aspects of swimming with a buddy, wild swimming can strengthen your friendship at the same time as deepening your connection with nature. There's the opportunity to chat before and afterwards, and maybe even when you're in the water. Plus, if you've arranged to meet a friend for a wild swim and it's in the diary, you're going to make sure you're there as you won't want to let them down.

## Go slow

Just before getting into cold water, some preparatory breathing work is a good idea, and puts you in a happy place before you swim. Keep that breathing going as you get into the water. Don't jump in; take it slowly, easing yourself into the water as you do your breathing cycles.

## Blood flow test

There is a test to see whether you're getting dangerously cold: try and bring your thumb and little finger together. If you can't manage to do this, it's because you don't have enough blood flow to activate those muscles, and you should get out of the water immediately.

## Get on your back

If you get into trouble in the water, try to get on to your back and take steady breaths. If you're on your back and you can inflate your lungs, you will float on the surface. You can also look for escape routes or for someone who could throw you something to hold on to.

## Beware Britain's most poisonous plant

When wild swimming, be careful where you get in and out. The hemlock water dropwort plant seems to be in all our waterways, ditches and lakes and even by the sea, and you could easily unknowingly grab a handful to help pull yourself out of the water. It looks benign, but it could kill; it contains a cocktail of chemicals that your body can't break down. If you get any of the sap in your bloodstream, you could be dead within three hours. Look out for its celery-like stalk and the parsley-like leaves and try to find another way in and out of the water. Other considerations: tides, strong currents, becoming entangled in vegetation, underwater obstacles, chemical interference plus environmental factors such as gravel beds where fish lay eggs. Assess at your own risk.

**Hemlock water dropwort**

### Don't swim for too long

The first few times you go wild swimming, it can be difficult to know when you've been in the water for long enough; the temptation is to stay in for longer than you should, risking your body getting too cold. If in doubt, it's probably best to get out – don't ever push it. This is where you need your friend, the one who ideally has some previous experience of wild swimming, to tell you that it's time to get out.

But this is the moment to savour – as it's when you emerge from the water that you feel the natural high most intensely.

## REWILDING REMINDER

- If you want to feel alive, spend a few minutes in cold, wild water – it will instantly change your mood; you will get out of the river, sea or lake feeling incredible.

- You will be exhilarated, energised, freer and lighter.

# PART TWO

# REDISCOVER

Do you want to feel human again?

In Part Two, you'll have the chance to rediscover skills that would have been essential for your ancestors' daily survival. You could say you're going to be rediscovering what it's like to be a human as these are the skills that we needed before we ever had microwaves, taps, kettles and fast-food delivery apps.

So many of the skills that your bloodline discovered, keeping them alive in the wild, have been forgotten by most. But I'm going to take you through those skills, showing you how to make a wild cup of tea, how to sleep under the moon and stars, as well as introducing you to foraging as well as how to use knives and axes.

This journey of rediscovery is going to give you a very real and tangible skill set, making you less reliant on modern technology, and able to thrive in the natural and modern world.

As you get outside and pick this stuff up, you'll also be enhancing your mental health, which is going to help you get through the day-to-day trials and tribulations of your everyday life. You'll be building your confidence and resilience while feeling calmer and more self-reliant.

# 15

# A WILD CUP OF TEA

How wild do you want to go with your tea today? Yes, there are different levels of wild cups of tea. Obviously, I'm here to encourage you to go as wild as you can. I promise you that the first time you make yourself a *truly* wild cup of tea it will taste extraordinary. There's nothing more delicious than that first sip of your very first wild cup of tea.

I can still taste my first wild brew, which I made while messing about in the woods as a teenager. It was mint tea, drunk out of an enamel cup, and made with mint that my friend and I had collected, which we threw into a pot and stirred for a while. It was crude but also divine. Hundreds of wild cups of mint tea later, I can tell you that this drink still tastes good. Anything that's made in the wild is always going to taste better than an ordinary, everyday mug of tea at home. As a Marine, I had some memorable cups of wild tea all over the world, from drinking chai tea with Afghans in the Hindu Kush mountains to milky, very sugary tea with high-level Pakistani military to some mind-blowingly fresh mint tea by the side of the road when travelling through Morocco.

## THE SLOWER THE BETTER

As great as the taste is, that's only one part of the whole experience, which is wonderfully slow. Even when you get the hang of it, making a wild cup of tea is never going to be a fast process, but somehow that's the point. I know we live in a world in which we want everything right now, but this is an opportunity to take your time.

If you're anything like me, you'll be enjoying your surroundings while you're making a wild cup of tea, and you won't want to rush. You'll be in the outdoors, in the fresh air, maybe listening to the chirping birds and the free-flowing water, and feeling a gentle breeze against your skin. If you're going to get the most from being in nature, you need to embrace the mindset of relaxing, taking your time and engaging with your landscape. When making a wild cup of tea, you won't have any alternative but to slow down and take it easy. And if you've chosen to make a calming wild tea – made from camomile or lime flowers, perhaps – you will feel very chilled indeed.

## EMPOWERED BY TEA

I remember how satisfying it was to make my first wild tea, and I would love you to experience that, too. It gives you a quiet confidence that never leaves you. You forage for the ingredients and create a drink that is safe to ingest – in this day and age, that's a rare thing. Everything comes out of a packet these days. Well, you're going to teach yourself that you don't need to rely on supermarket teabags. You can enjoy a hot drink in the wild with herbs or berries you've foraged.

Learning how to make a cup of wild tea will show you that you can fend for yourself in the outdoors, that you're not completely reliant on all the comforts and technologies that make our home and work lives pretty simple. This is about as far away as possible from running a tap at home, boiling a kettle and grabbing a teabag from the cupboard.

As I've already said, there are different levels of wildness to wild tea. Some days, you might choose to undertake every single part of the tea-making process; other days, you might choose to simplify the process (you might, for instance, bring water from home, but flavour the tea with something you've foraged and light the fire to boil it on). And if you're living in a block of flats, and can't source water or make a fire today, you can still go wilder than a mug of English Breakfast. Certainly run the tap in your home and boil the kettle, but do go out and forage for a herb, berry or some other plant to flavour your drink.

So, what exactly does making wild tea involve?

## HOW TO MAKE A CUP OF WILD TEA

To make a truly wild cup of tea means sourcing, filtering and purifying the water; preparing and starting a fire; and foraging for the natural ingredients to flavour it. You can use the skills laid out in this chapter for far more than making a wild cup of tea. For example, if your water bottle is running low when you're outdoors, that's not a problem if you know how to source, filter and purify water; you can top up your supplies from a spring or stream. And knowing how to make a basic criss-cross fire lay (imagine a game of wild Jenga that goes up in flames) is useful for more than just boiling water.

## Sourcing water

Hunting for fresh, clean water is a great part of exploring the outdoors. If you're not sure which direction to walk in to find a watercourse, climb up somewhere high, such as up a small hill, as that will help you with your natural navigation. What can you see from your viewpoint? And what can you hear? On a still day, when there's not much wind, you might be able to hear a river or stream, so follow that sound and see what you discover. I'm always keen to get off the beaten track to find the cleanest water, but that obviously comes with risk, so only do what you're comfortable with.

You're looking for clear, fast-flowing and oxygenated water. The faster, the better, as if a river or stream is flowing slowly, it's more likely to be full of nasties or germs that could make you unwell. You can tell if water's well-oxygenated as there will be small bubbles rising to the surface. Water will tend be at its most oxygenated when flowing quickly over rocks; when the water drops, over the side of the rocks, it will pull oxygen down with it, and that comes to the surface as bubbles.

Ideally, you want to find a spring, as that will be the cleanest water you'll find for your wild cup of tea. The further you are from the source, the more likely the water is to come into contact with debris, dead animals, and animals' faeces and urine. Water from a spring is also likely to have been naturally purified underground, but you will still need to filter and purify it before drinking.

Once you've found a watercourse, look around to see what sort of vegetation is growing nearby? If there's nothing growing by the river that's a big warning sign that the water is full of chemicals and you won't want to drink it. Look out for reeds – they are an indication of a healthy river and act as a natural filtration system.

Before collecting any water, walk at least 100 metres upstream to ensure there aren't any cows, sheep or even humans adding faeces and urine, which would be a big bacterial risk. If you're in any doubt about the cleanliness of the water, keep looking. Always be prepared to walk for a little longer to be sure you're going to be collecting the cleanest water in the area.

It could be that you decide to capture rainwater, which is absolutely fine, but you'll still need to filter and purify it. And remember, the water's only ever going to be as clean as whatever you're collecting it in – be that a poncho, a tarpaulin or a bucket, etc. Don't use stagnant water that's been sitting around for a long time.

When collecting water, always stand downstream from your bottle or canteen. If you stand upstream, you could disturb the mud or silt on the riverbed, some of which could end up in your container. Even if the water looks clean and clear, don't be tempted to take a sip from it; there are a couple of steps you need to go through before you do that.

## Filtering water

Now you've got your water, do a quick inspection to make sure it's clean and clear of debris. If it isn't, tip it back and collect some more. To make the water safe to drink, and to get rid of any small pieces of mud, leaves and anything else, you must pass it through a filter. I recommend something called a Millbank Bag, which I always carry with me in the outdoors. While some people make their own material filters – perhaps from an old pair of jeans – I would encourage you to stick with a Millbank Bag. Before using the Millbank Bag, you'll need to soak it in water for a few minutes; this expands the fibres and creates a tighter mesh that will catch more.

Once you've given the bag a chance to expand, hang it on a tree and pour your collected water through, collecting all the drips below. You can pour your water through the bag twice, or even three times, depending on your personal comfort. This might take ten minutes or even longer, but it's not exactly taxing and shouldn't be rushed. Don't ever be tempted to squeeze the bag, thinking that will speed the process up, as that risks opening up some of the fibres and letting nasties through. Let the bag do its job. Also be prepared to lose some of the water while doing this; you might even need to go back to the spring or stream to collect more water (for that reason, I would suggest doing the filtering nearby to save yourself having to walk too far).

There are plenty of gadgets on the market for filtering water – there are even straws that allow you to drink straight from a stream. My concern about some of these items is how do you know when they are no longer working? Maybe when you get diarrhoea halfway up a mountain? That's when you'll know it's gone wrong. Whereas the humble Millbank Bag is very dependable; after use, you turn it inside out, wash it, leave it to dry and then it's ready to go again.

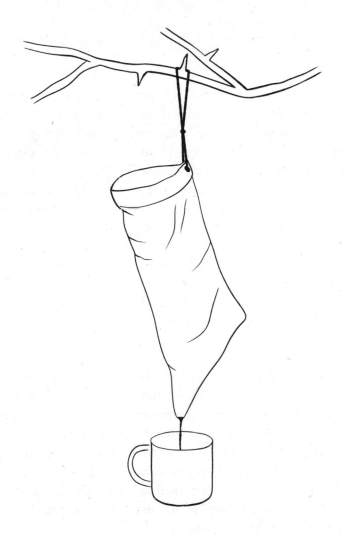

**A Millbank Bag filtering water**

**Purifying water**

In the Marines, we were heavily reliant on sterilisation tablets. They would kill anything nasty in the water – thus keeping you alive – but it made the water taste like a swimming pool. And if you don't read the tablet instructions carefully and get the dosage wrong, there's a danger of doing yourself an awful lot of harm.

If you suspect there are chemicals in the watercourse you've located, then go ahead and use other chemicals, i.e., sterilisation tablets, to purify it. But what we're talking about in this chapter is a *therapeutic* cup of tea that's going to make you feel good about yourself, and I don't think that means water purified with tablets. In the Marines we often didn't have the luxury of an open fire to boil the water and kill off most of the germs. But, if you're able to light a fire, you should be able to make your filtered water safe and create a truly wild cup of tea.

Bring your wild water to a rolling boil – that's not just a few bubbles, but a proper boil. You don't have to boil it for longer than five minutes – as some people might suggest – to kill all the germs, and after five minutes you'll just start losing your precious, collected water through evaporation.

## STARTING A FIRE

What could possibly be more primal than starting a fire in the wild? You can't help but think to yourself: "I can provide for myself, just as my ancestors did." Every time I teach someone how to start a fire, their whole face lights up (I'm talking metaphorically here, so don't imagine their head going up in flames). They're always thrilled at having started a fire.

While you could boil the water on a camping gas stove or a bioethanol stove (which is quiet and clean-burning, so better for the environment), doing it on an open fire is the wilder choice.

Later in the book, I discuss we can all connect around a fire, and I also explain how to make different types of fire (pages 189–94).

Here, we'll focus on the criss-cross fire. A criss-cross fire burns quickly, allowing you to rapidly boil water, ideal for making a wild cup of tea.

## Fire prep

Find a suitable spot to start a fire in the outdoors. You should be in an opening, away from *any* trees or vegetation that could potentially catch fire, and more than 100 metres from a river. And you should always have the landowner's permission before starting a fire.

Consider the **wind** – which way is it blowing? You could drop some dust, or maybe some ash if you've had another fire, nearby to see where it goes. But that's not going to tell you much if there's only a gentle breeze. A better method of determining wind direction is to lick the back of your hand and move it around to see where the wind is coming from that cools the wetness down. The reason the wind direction matters is because you want to position the platform so that the air will flow directly into the fire.

As I learned in the Marines, planning is key to almost everything, including making a fire. Before you light your fire, you need to collect all the natural material, twigs and pieces of wood you're going to need. What's known as tinder is light, fluffy, soft material that burns easily, and will get the initial flame going. Then you'll need kindling, and then larger pieces of wood. I go into this in much greater detail in Part Three, page 175.

## Building a platform

Now you've got your fire spot and all your materials, you need to create a platform.

The platform will lift your firewood off the invisible moisture layer that sits on the forest floor throughout the year, even in summer. The moment you put your wood down on the ground, it will start to get damp, making it that bit harder to start your fire, so try to keep all your firewood off the floor at all times. Having a platform, with gaps between the pieces of wood, will create channels for air to flow underneath and through and up into the fire. A constant air flow is needed as a fire needs to breathe, just as you and I do.

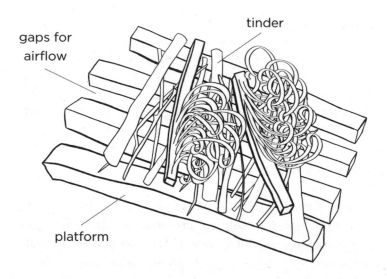

tinder

gaps for
airflow

platform

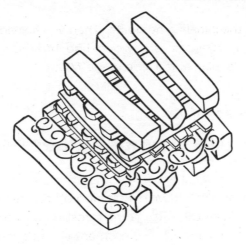

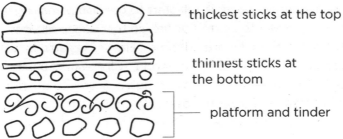

thickest sticks at the top

thinnest sticks at
the bottom

platform and tinder

## Criss-cross fire

Now it's time to start building the fire. At the base will be
your tinder, on top of which you'll place your kindling.

Start with wood that's about the size of your finger, and
gradually and carefully add larger pieces of wood. Put
each piece on in a criss-cross fashion, as if you're setting
up a wild game of Jenga.

As with the platform, this pattern maximises the air space
and allows you to create a thermal column for the fire to
climb up and out of. It's going to be a bit wobbly at first,
but find a way to balance the wood. Be patient and you'll
get there in the end.

Now your fire is ready to be lit. You *could* light it with matches or a regular lighter or – to be truly wild – by friction. This part of the process is covered on pages 195–201.

## NATURAL FLAVOURS AND REMEDIES

I *love* mint tea. **Mint** is easy to identify, so you can be sure you're not poisoning yourself, and it smells and tastes delicious (especially if it's your first wild cup of tea).

**Pine needle** tea will give you a lovely clementine, citric and orangey taste, and it's full of vitamin C, which is great for your immune system (and after the tea is cooled, you can pour some on a cut or wound as it has antiseptic qualities and will help to keep it clean).

Another favourite of mine is **rosemary** tea, which is strongly perfumed and has a very relaxing effect on the body. You can find that in most garden centres.

Or you could try making tea with **camomile**, which calms and soothes your central nervous system. While you can buy camomile in shops or online, you can also find it in the wild. It grows anywhere that the sun is shining and there's good quality soil. **Lime flower** can also be a calming tea.

I make a lot of **blackberry leaf** tea and can recommend **alehoof** tea.

The inner bark of the **willow tree** can be soaked in water and used to make a cup of tea with anti-inflammatory and pain-killing properties.

You can also make tea with **St John's wort**, which gives off a lemony smell and is a natural anti-depressant (but you're not meant to have any if you're already taking anti-depressant medication).

If I've got diarrhoea, I'll have a cup of **wild acorn** tea – it's full of tannins that tan the stomach lining, sealing it and stopping liquid from passing through. It also tastes great.

One of the advantages of taking wild medicine is that you can do it on an empty stomach as it often works in harmony with your body. That's not possible with modern medicine, which is full of bulking agents – such as silicone and chalk – to make the pills shelf stable.

If you want to go wild but don't yet have the confidence to forage for yourself, then off-the-shelf herbal teas are widely available. While the herbs aren't as fresh as they've been dried, they're still potent. So, pack a teabag or two of your preferred herbal tea in your backpack when you head out on your next wild adventure.

# Preparing the plant

When preparing any wild tea, crush the plant in your fingers so you get maximum cellular damage. That ensures it will release its compounds when you put it in hot water.

When crushed **mint** is in hot water it will release its lovely volatile oils, which we can taste and feel, which clear our airways, and which gently stimulate the linings of our guts.

A wild cup of tea can be medicinal, as combining forest herbs with hot water is a great way of ingesting complementary medicines.

Whenever one of my old injuries starts to flare up, I head into the wild looking for **meadowsweet**. I'll chop the root very finely and add hot, but not boiling, water. It's full of salicylic acid, which is an active ingredient for aspirin. I will drink this tea on a regular basis and very soon everything calms down.

**REWILDING REMINDER**

- There's nothing more delicious than your first wild cup of tea.

- But wild tea doesn't just taste good – it makes you feel good.

- It gives you a quiet confidence, as it shows you that you can fend for yourself in the wild and that you're not completely dependent on modern comforts and technologies.

# 6

# SLEEPING UNDER THE MOON & STARS

The moon, the stars and the night sky have helped me though some hard times in my life, through periods of extreme duress, to the point where I feel I have a relationship with the moon. Sleeping under the stars is a magical experience, but people often focus on the constellations and forget about the moon. Depending on where I am in the world, and the level of light pollution, I'll only be able to see certain stars, but on a clear night I'll always be able to look up and see the moon wherever I may be. The moon's always going to be there, and that's very reassuring to me.

Early on in my first tour in Afghanistan, the landscape felt very alien, added to which I didn't yet know much about the culture, even though we had been briefed before leaving Britain. I couldn't have felt further from home.

When you're on sentry duty in your forward operating base or patrol base at night, with just one another Marine or alone with your thoughts, you realise what a dangerous situation you're in. You're completely surrounded by the enemy and you're the last line of defence while your mates are sleeping. There was a constant threat all around us, and I knew that if I lost focus for a moment the enemy could overrun us.

On those dark, unsettling nights, there was always something comforting about the moon, especially if I was feeling homesick. I would look up at the moon, wondering whether loved ones in Britain were doing the same – despite being thousands of miles apart, we would have been sharing that experience of watching the moon and stars. The moon was like a familiar face, and I used it to self-soothe. However, I always had to be careful that, while looking up at the moon, it wasn't lighting up my face, as that could have made me a white, bright target on top of a roof.

I've never forgotten how the moon got me through some of those nights. I'm eternally grateful. Ever since that tour, I've felt a connection with the moon. No matter where I am in the world, I know the moon will always be there to comfort me when I'm feeling low or anxious. It's one constant in an otherwise fast-changing, uncertain world.

Some people love the sea, others the mountains and vast, epic landscapes; what gets me going is a lovely bit of woodland, though sadly that's becoming rarer and rarer in the United Kingdom, where only a tiny percentage of ancient woodland is left (it's still out there, but you just have to know where to look). I was 14 years old when I went wild camping for the first time, and my passion for sleeping under the stars has only grown since then.

## OPEN TO THE SKY

If you're going to be spending the night outside, I feel it's important to actually be able to see the stars and the moon. I believe that if you're under a tarpaulin, with a good view of what's going on around you, you will go to sleep as part of that landscape and wake up as part of that landscape, too. If you are in a tent, keep the door open so you have the view of the landscape and of as much of the sky as possible. If you shut yourself away in a tent with the zip up, you might as well be in your house – you're camping but not really camping. Being able to see what's going on adds to your feeling of calm – hearing a noise outside from within a closed-up tent can cause you to conjure up ideas of what's on the other side of the canvas. You start imagining big, hungry predators. The reality, of course, is that it's probably just a mouse or some other small animal going for a 3am stroll.

## BE CAREFREE

Before you go to sleep, look up at the moon and stars one more time. You're part of the landscape tonight; embrace that, as it's a wonderful feeling that you won't get from sleeping in your bed at home. If you're going through a hard time and feeling low, you would be forgiven for thinking, "I'm such a small part of this universe, who's going to miss me when I'm gone?" That's easily done, and I've been there, but it's a negative approach to take and should be resisted. Instead, wonder at the stars and the world around you.

Sleeping under the stars, you will feel completely connected to nature. Tell yourself you're living your best life, which is out in the natural world. You're away from everything artificial and away from the hustle, gossip and nonsense. We spend so much time thinking about what everyone thinks of us, and how society expects us to look and behave, but when you're out under the stars, the realisation hits you: "I don't care." Sleeping under the stars, you realise how it's better to embrace being you, and to do whatever makes *you* happy, even if people are going to judge you for it. Say it again: "I don't care."

# SLEEP WELL

Being outside under the stars is a chance to get some good sleep. Sleep has a massive effect on my mental health, and will have on yours too. Occasionally, something in my life will trip or trigger me and I'll get bouts of sleep deprivation. Before long, I'll have bags under my eyes, be feeling irritable and my wellbeing will be on the slide. When that happens, I know I need to quickly get a grip on myself and pull myself back from that downward cycle. As soon as I feel that happening, I introduce a stricter sleep hygiene routine, such as laying off the caffeine, winding things down generally and being strict about not blasting myself with blue light and other stimulus by looking at my phone just before bed.

But the best way of rebooting everything is to spend a night or two out in the wild. Sleeping under the stars is the ultimate detox.

If you can get away from the grime and grind of the city, leave all the smog and business behind and retreat to a woodland, you're going to be getting the best quality oxygen – think about all the fresh oxygen those trees emit. Yes, you'll probably end up waking up earlier than usual, at sunrise or just before with the dawn chorus. But you should also be going to sleep earlier than you would do at home, which is just what your body wants to do, rather than being kept awake by artificial light. At home, your circadian rhythm – when your body wants to sleep based on light levels – is likely to be all out of whack. You're probably going to bed much later than when your body naturally wants to sleep. Spend a night or two outside, take the opportunity to sleep in a more natural way, and you will feel all the better for the experience.

## LEARN AND GROW

One of the many things I adore about sleeping outside is that nature holds you to account. If you're at a point in your life where you're procrastinating or only doing things half-heartedly – starting things but never finishing them – going on a camping trip can snap you out of that. This is because if you haven't secured your shelter properly, and the top gets ripped off in the middle of the night by a gust of wind, you're going to have to get out of your sleeping bag, scramble through the forest to find it and set it back up again. I can guarantee that's an experience you won't want to repeat.

Being in nature also promotes a growth mindset that will help you to deal with situations in everyday life. In the wild, you can't just park your problem, or say you can't cope or that it's not your problem; you have to immediately stop and address the issue. Maybe you're using avoidance techniques in other parts of your life; in the wild, that's not going to work. If it starts to rain, you can't go into denial – you can't say, "Well, I'm just going to stand here and get wet." You will need to quickly do something about it, such as putting your waterproofs on and perhaps finding somewhere to shelter. You're accountable for yourself and your equipment, and if you're in a group you all look out for each other.

Nature forces us to learn quickly, and it can be our greatest teacher. I haven't always got it right first time, and there have been frustrations and failures along the way, but I've understood the need to learn quickly if I'm going to look after myself in the wild.

In the woods, you often find you have to stop and face what's happening to you in your life. Sometimes you feel as though the whole world is against you, but maybe once you pause to reflect on what's going on you might discover that the problem is you. Looking inwards can be the most difficult and painful part of growth. There's a tendency among all of us – a danger even – to think that life is unfair, to believe you're always the victim. That's a difficult pattern of behaviour to break free from, but it can be done – and sleeping in the wild might help start to get you there.

I appreciate that this might sound a little contradictory, but while nature holds you to account it also sets you free. I love the freedom of sleeping outside. I'm in charge, with no-one telling me what's right and what's wrong. To a certain extent – as you obviously want to be warm and safe – you can make it up as you go along, and therein lies the adventure. Sleeping under the stars, and feeling the freedom of being in nature, you really find your own headspace, which is what makes it so incredible.

But you don't have to go alone. Sleeping under the stars with a friend is a great bonding experience. It also helps to keep you a little safer as two brains tend to be better than one. However, if you do go alone, always let someone know beforehand where you're heading. For this, use technology to your advantage – for example, the phone app "what3words" allows others to find your exact location to the nearest few metres.

# WHEN TO GO

Sleeping under the stars doesn't have to be just a summer, fair-weather activity – I encourage you to go out at all times of year. While we all love the feeling of the summer sun on our face, and of course it's going to be easier and more comfortable sleeping wild during the warmer months, you'll learn to appreciate the summer even more if you also try sleeping out in the winter. You get a better understanding of the seasons when you sleep outside throughout the year.

When it's cold, you're also building your resilience. And when you come home and slide into a hot bath, you will have that wonderful feeling of accomplishment. I'm not suggesting for a moment that you should beast yourself and put yourself in extreme discomfort, as being outside should be pleasurable rather than a painful, miserable experience. So long as you have the right clothing and equipment, you can take on the challenge and prove to yourself that you can rough it if you have to – you'll certainly learn to appreciate your fire-making skills and your sleeping bag all the more.

While I slept under the stars a fair bit before becoming a Marine, the military gave me a crash course in acute, high-stress, high-discomfort camping. It's known as "aggressive camping" for a reason. You're under duress. You're having to wake every few hours to do sentry duty, looking out into the darkness to stop the enemy from running through your position. In training, we had to experience the "wet and dry routine", which separates the wheat from the chaff. Every couple of hours, you're woken up and expected to remove your dry clothing for a full set of soaked-through clothes. This could take place on Dartmoor in the winter, when it might be minus 12 degrees Celsius. When it was that cold, the wet trousers were often frozen solid, and you would have to wrap them round the base of a tree to try to give them some shape before putting them on against your bare skin. I might have then had to lie on the forest floor for two hours. It was brutal and disorientating. I would make myself do press-ups every now and then, to keep me alert and to get the blood pumping around my muscles. That was camping on a different level, but it taught me how to camp anywhere.

Don't take this as encouragement to go aggressive camping – I don't think you'd like it. But I do think you'll have a good time sleeping under the stars. Remember, when you're sleeping outside, it's not about surviving, but thriving.

## STOP TO TAKE IN THE "GREEN CATHEDRAL"

When I first step into a piece of woodland that's new to me, I'll pause at the edge for a few moments. I might have approached it from open, rolling countryside, with big views, and now suddenly nature is up close. I like to acclimatise to my surroundings, including the changes in light, the sounds and the smells. I suggest that you do the same. As you pause, you can start thinking about what happens next and where you'll go from here. In that same situation, our ancestors would have been thinking, "Is something going to come charging through the trees at me?" While you won't have that issue to consider, you could nevertheless look around to see if anyone else is in the woods. If someone is already camping there, or if they already have their hammock up, I would move on as I don't want to be disturbing them.

In that moment, try to enjoy the process of slowing down and taking it all in. Think of a woodland as a green cathedral. When you walk into an actual cathedral, you don't just bowl in there; you stop, look up and around and take your time. You take in the magnificence of the place. I recommend you take the same approach with woodland. I'm not an overly spiritual person, but when I do this it feels like I'm asking permission to be there (I'm not quite sure who I'm asking). It's not my habitat, this is where other animals live, and I have to respect that and not just charge around as if it's my domain. Those first few moments in a new woodland provide an opportunity for mindfulness, for considering your senses.

From the moment you step in, you should be asking yourself, if rain comes, where's the best tree around for shelter. Start to think about the location of possible water sources and also where you might harvest wood for your fire or forage for food.

There's a lot of information to take in, and acclimatising to woodlands doesn't happen instantly. Take your time, and remember to enjoy the process.

## ALWAYS GET PERMISSION

As teenagers, my friend Chris and I used to get a buzz from wild camping somewhere we probably shouldn't have been. We didn't have the landowner's permission, and in the morning there was the thrill of knowing we had got away with it. I'm not suggesting that you do the same.

Before you sleep anywhere you should always seek the landowner's permission, as you're not going to find the experience very relaxing if you get woken up in the middle of the night by an angry landowner.

Do some research before you go and look at the local laws to see what you can and can't do (which might change depending on the time of the year). As a general rule, wild camping is permitted in Scotland and in a few places in England and Wales, such as Dartmoor National Park which has specific wild camping sites (but is often tolerated in most other places). Have a look at what's possible near you.

## LOCATION, LOCATION, LOCATION

In the Marines, we would sometimes live inside a hedge for days. In the civilian world, that's known as stealth camping. For us, it was observation position work. Up to four of us lived in cramped conditions inside a hedge or inside a bank, after digging our way in. While no one could spot us, we could see what was going on, which made it perfect for monitoring enemy movements and sending that information back to an operations room so they could build up a better picture and decide whether to mount a strike. However, I don't think that you're going to have an enjoyable time in a hedge. There is also a very real danger of potential disaster if you are stealth camping on land which is used for hunting at night (lamping).

When choosing where to sleep outside, you're naturally going to want to be somewhere beautiful, where you can enjoy the view; but there are other factors to consider too, such as where might be the safest and the most comfortable spot.

## Weather

Choosing the right location is crucial, and it is very important to think about the orientation to the wind. You don't want to be at the top of a hill or mountain, where you'll be exposed whatever the wind direction; but you don't want to be at the bottom either as, although you'll find water there, that's where the cold collects. So somewhere halfway up a hill or mountain is never a bad shout – depending in where the wind is coming from. If it rains and you get wet, you will lose heat 25 to 30 times faster if you're in the wind.

Many of the world's greatest survivalists and explorers have come from Britain, and that's probably because we don't have any weather constants. You could experience sunshine, rain, wind and snow on any given day, and you need to be prepared for all those eventualities. Our seasons are increasingly unpredictable, with the only guarantee being that the leaves will fall off the trees at some point.

## Water

You'll want to be close, but not too close, to a water source. Finding clean running water is key to sleeping under the stars. It gives you the ability to cook, wash yourself and top up your water bottle. It also means you can put out your fire (should you choose to have one).

See page 82 for locating water, but don't camp on the bank of a stream or river, or within a few metres of any water source, as you could end up damaging the environment you're enjoying – if you leave anything behind, or dig a latrine, it will eventually find its way into the water. Ideally, you want to be some distance from the water but close enough so you can easily benefit from it.

## Vegetation

Look around you carefully and try to find a decent clearing. As much as you can, try to ensure you're not damaging any plants of scientific value.

Areas of woodland with split or broken trees – also known as widow-makers – are an absolute no-go as you risk being squashed during the night.

If you're in woodland with a high canopy, please be very careful that you're not setting up camp beneath any trees that are barely holding themselves up. If the wind suddenly whips through at night, then the tree and you and your hammock could come crashing down. Another warning sign is when there's a fallen tree nearby, as if one tree has toppled another could join it shortly.

If a woodland is very wild, you might not see any chain-sawed tree stumps, which tells you it hasn't been managed for a very long time. That's all the more reason to think about what's going on above you and where will be safe to sleep.

As I walk, my eyes pick up on all the dead wood, and how it's fallen. Where I live, the prevailing south-westerly wind causes all storm-damaged branches and trees to fall in one direction, and determines my choice of camp on the northern side, where I'm further away from a potential domino effect.

If I can find one, I like to bed down on a raised spot on the edge of a woodland, as you'll get extra light. Look for a flat spot as no one likes to sleep on a slope. And keep away from any known animal tracks, where animals might walk to water or come through in a hurry.

I wrote in the forest bathing chapter about the importance of not always going back to the same spot again and again, as that could potentially damage the trees; this also applies to when you're sleeping under the stars. I know it's tempting to return to the place where you had a great experience, but think of this as a reason to discover new places, which is fun in itself.

## SLEEP SYSTEM

Sometimes I'll chose to sleep on the ground. But more often than not, if the trees around allow it, I'll sleep in a hammock. You get that amazing feeling of being cocooned in your sleeping bag inside your hammock, but to still feel completely immersed in the woodland.

In a hammock, you will probably wake up around first light, and your eyes will slowly open as the dawn chorus gets going in the background. You might spot a deer just metres away from you, or a badger, or whatever else is going on in the woods.

# Tarp top tips

While you might feel as though a tent is going to offer you more protection from the weather, you could compromise and invest in a tarpaulin – which won't cost you much – this may just bring you closer to nature.

Another reason to choose a tarp over a tent is that it packs down pretty small, making it easier to carry.

## Options

I've got a tarpaulin that's 4.5 metres by 3 metres, which gives me lots of room underneath, but they come in a range of sizes. The classic, camouflaged British military poncho is a popular choice among many wild campers. Incredibly versatile and durable, the poncho can put up with a lot and has saved my bacon more times than I can remember. It's so strong it can double up as a stretcher and hold the weight of a man in full armour who has just been hit and needs to be evacuated. The poncho's also inexpensive; I really rate it.

## Preparation

If you end up setting up camp in the dying light, things will get lost, so put on a head-torch before the light goes. I suggest taking things out of your bag in the order you need them. If you're not going to be using something just yet, keep it in your bag until you do.

## Tarpology

Sounds like some kind of dark art, doesn't it? However, it's actually describing the practice of complicated configurations that people like to form with their tarpaulin, as if they're doing wild origami.

The tarpaulin is extremely versatile, and you can quickly and easily make different shapes and sizes. By adjusting and folding the tarpaulin in different ways you can manage numerous scenarios and various weather conditions. But try to keep things simple, as to attempt anything too complex and challenging goes against wanting to get back to basics in nature.

As a nature-lover, I recommend an open configuration which provides a widescreen view of what's going on around you. This also means you get the last of the evening light and the first of the morning sun. If the wind picks up, or a storm is coming in, you can change it to more of a tent shape, which provides more protection from the elements. Also make sure that when you're underneath your tarp that you're not touching it, as, depending on air flow, condensation may build and leave you feeling wet – and that won't be comfortable.

## Wind

When choosing your tarp configuration, consider the wind. You don't want to create a wind tunnel, nor do you want a sail effect where your tarpaulin is constantly catching the wind and trying to take off.

## Open configuration tarp set-up

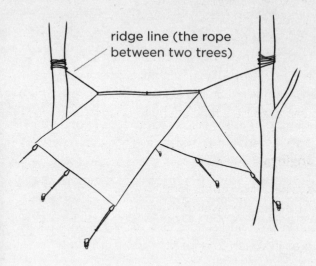

ridge line (the rope between two trees)

You will need to maintain tension in your tarp as this will help shed wind and rain. Aim to keep it taut and picture perfect. Adding some give will also protect nature – if your ridge line is putting large amounts of pressure through small diameter tree trunks, you're likely to damage them.

## Accessories

Bungee cords can be great for putting up a tarpaulin. We used them in the Marines as they are fast and easy and have some give in them. But if you ever find yourself making adjustments to tarpaulins in the middle of the night, there's always a danger that the bungee could ping back and whack you in the eye.

From experience, I can tell you that that's going to hurt, so you might be better off using rope or paracord. Losing pegs is a hazard of being in the wild, so count how many you use when putting up the tarp, and then count them back into the bag. If this is new to you, you might want to practise in your back garden or in a nearby area of green space. This can even be a fun activity to do with your kids.

## Belongings

Always keeping your belongings off the ground, which will have a layer of moisture. Wait until the tarpaulin is up and secure, providing you with a safe, dry area in which to unpack.

# Sleeping bag top tips

## Weight

Travel light, freeze at night – there's a lot of truth in that. When you're choosing a sleeping bag, I recommend going for the most robust choice, even if that one's heavier and doesn't pack up as small as other options. Prioritise sleep and comfort.

The heavier bag comes with the psychological comfort of knowing you're going to get a good night's sleep. When I'm feeling depleted and tired, I can always push on, knowing that I'm going to get six hours, even more, when I set up camp and get into my bag. Invest in a bag that won't fail you.

## Two-in-one

While you can get some super-lightweight bags that scrunch down to almost nothing, I would only use one of those on an adventure outside Britain where it's warmer at night. It can get very cold at night in Britain.

One possibility you might want to consider is the two-in-one system, where you're buying a medium weight and a lightweight bag in a set.

In winter, you put the two bags together, and when it's a little warmer at night you can just use the medium bag and then just the light one in the heat of summer. A foam roll mat will add insulation and cushioning.

## Construction

My experience of using sleeping bags with synthetic filling is that they are generally more robust than one insulated with down.

Down bags can be very expensive to buy and then you have the additional cost of getting them dry-cleaned; synthetic bags can be thrown in the washing and drying machines.

## My favourite

The bag I use in winter is the British Artic sleeping bag. Fully insulated and lined, this out-performs any other bag in terms of its durability and ability to hold your body's heat.

## Accessories

Whenever I sleep under the stars, I take my military Gore-Tex bivvy bag. Sometimes I'll go out into the wild with everything already set up, with my sleeping bag already inside the bivvy bag, as then I can set up camp very quickly, just unrolling it.

If it all goes wrong in the night – if the tarpaulin is ripped off by a gust of wind or the hammock falls on to the forest floor – as long as I'm inside that waterproof bivvy bag, all will be well.

# SLEEP SPACE

I've already shared my tips on setting up a hammock on page 30, but if you're camping overnight, rather than just forest bathing for a little while, there's a little more involved.

Remember, your bedspace should be sacred and you've got to look after it. When you've spent all day on the trail, you'll want to get into a clean, dry bag. Only when I'm just about to go to sleep do I get my sleeping bag, and anything else I need for the night, out of my bag. That's because I don't want millions of creepy-crawlies, and other bits and pieces, getting into the bag or hammock and disturbing me during the night.

Before you get into your sleeping bag, you might wish to roll up the bottom of your trouser legs, which will have picked up loads of rubbish and mud throughout the day. That will help prevent mud and other debris from getting into your bag.

Being in nature is often about taking your time, and working at your own pace, so don't rush when getting everything set up for the night. Arrange things just how you want them, in a way that will make you as comfortable as possible.

Hammocks aren't the easiest things to get in and out of, so make sure you go to the loo before you get in and settle down for the night. If you like to sip water throughout the night, you could suspend a bottle just above you so you can easily reach it without getting in and out of your hammock.

## My bedtime routine

I have a routine when getting into my sleeping bag, which I stick to whether I'm going to be spending the night on the forest floor or in a hammock.

- I take my coat of, scrunch it up and place near the hammock.

- I remove my knife from my belt and place it in my boots or in a little bag which is suspended above.

- I put my boots at an angle so I can easily get back into them, should I need to in the dark.

As a Marine in the jungles of Belize, you had to think about turning your boots upside down and putting them on sticks. One night, I forgot to do that and I was just about to put my right boot on in the morning when I noticed a big claw. If I had put my foot inside, the crab could have taken my toe off. But in Britain everything's relatively benign and you don't have to worry. The worst thing that might happen is that a great big slug could climb into one of your shoes, and you'll get a nasty surprise in the morning (as will the poor slug).

- Everything I don't need when in the hammock, I stow away in my bag and out of trouble. Check all the zips are done up on the bag (so no slugs will get in).

- Once inside the sleeping bag, it's time to get naked. I strip down completely to let the bag do what it's designed to do: loft and trap a big bubble of heat around you.

  If you sleep fully clothed, I guarantee you're going to be grumbling in the morning that you were really cold during the night. And that will be because you didn't let the bag do its job. Your clothes don't have the same ability to lock in heat. If dressed, you will sweat inside your clothes and the bag won't be able to do its job properly so you are more likely to get cold.

Getting naked wasn't always an option in the Marines, and not for any modesty reasons but because sometimes you only had time for a couple of hours' sleep, and you didn't want to cut into that by getting undressed and then dressed again. You also had to be ready for the real possibility that you would have to break out of your bag in the middle of the night, grab your rifle and fight. Depending on the situation, we would sleep in trainers or slippers with a hard sole. Sometimes we would sleep fully clothed and booted, with our boots wrapped in potato sacks or plastic bags. Other nights we did something called hot-bagging – which was about as unpleasant as it sounds – when you leave your bag to go on duty and the person who had just finished sentry duty would get in to benefit from your body heat trapped inside.

To avoid sweating excessively, I would suggest only wearing any thermal base layers when you feel as though you really need them. Personally, I only like to

wear thermals (long-sleeved top and long johns) when I
know I'm going to be static for a while – such as in camp
– or in the depths of winter. If it's really cold, I'll put my
thermals at the bottom of my sleeping bag so I can put
them on if the temperature drops dramatically during the
night, which will probably be around 3am or 4am when
you definitely won't want to be getting out of your bag.
Consider buying thermals made from Merino wool as while
they don't wick away sweat as efficiently as pieces made
from modern fibres, they don't tend to smell anything like
as bad. Being in nature is no excuse for being stinky.

You might want to fold your clothes up and put them
between your sleeping bag and the bivvy bag. That
will keep your clothes dry and they will also be at body
temperature when you put them back on in the morning –
a win-win. Put a fresh pair of socks at the bottom of your
sleeping bag – I still get very excited about fresh socks,
and other former soldiers out there will know what I
mean, as putting them on always feels amazing, especially
when they're warm.

You'll struggle to find a better pillow than a decent quality
woollen jumper, which I take off just before getting into
my hammock. Depending on the temperature and the
type of bag you have, you might want to put the hood
round your head, Egyptian mummy-style, though of
course always ensuring your mouth and nose are exposed
so you can breathe easily.

In the summer, you may not need a fire to keep warm, so
consider not lighting one (though there are other reasons
for wanting a fire, such as reconnecting while having real
conversations, which I explore in a later chapter). Not
sleeping next to a fire allows for a better wild experience
and encounters with animals – it's more of a stealth-like

way to experience nature. You're not imposing yourself on nature, as we often do as humans. You can lie in comfort in your hammock or under your tarp and watch the wildlife moving around you.

## WHAT AND HOW TO PACK

Don't just stuff a few bits into your bag a few minutes before you set off. Put some time – and thought – into what you pack before going on an overnighting adventure. Packing is a key skill in the outdoors: what you take, and where you put each item, can have an impact on how much you enjoy being with nature.

I know there are some people who go super-lightweight and boast they only have six kilograms on their backs. But I think if you're planning on doing some exploring in the wild, and then sleeping outside, you're going to need a few more items to make the trip easier and more comfortable. You could end up carrying around 15 kilograms, once you've taken into account water, food and kit. As a Marine, I used to have even more weight on my back, while also holding a weapon, so I'm very comfortable with the bag I carry now when going on adventures in the wild. While you may not have the same Commando conditioning, you will find that carrying a slightly heavier bag gets easier over time and is also a good workout, so you'll be getting in some cardio fitness as well as re-wilding yourself.

For an overnight trip, a 45-litre backpack should give you enough room for all your kit. Look for a bag with a large centre compartment, that you can load up with your stuff, and zippable side pouches. In training, I had a pretty sadistic sergeant who would hammer us if any zips were on show, which the weather could get into. That has stayed with me, and I still take pride in the flaps being down, covering the zips. Everything's neat and tidy. You could get a rain cover that goes over the whole bag. As an actual rain cover, it will probably let you down, but it's useful for when you're pushing through the undergrowth or thick woodland as everything just brushes off. It stops vegetation from catching and snagging on your bag. If you don't have a cover on, you can stop straps flying about and getting everywhere by securing them with fabric tape.

If your bag has chest and waist straps, use them. I wear the waist strap above my belt, so the weight of the pack is spread across my hips. If the waist strap is fixed too low, the weight of the pack will hang off the shoulders. I'm happy to have the weight low on my hips and back, but some people do prefer to have the weight loaded up around their shoulders; you'll soon discover what's most comfortable for you. Using the chest strap will help conserve your energy, as you won't have to keep pulling your shoulders forward to counter the weight of the pack.

## MY PACKING ROUTINE

Before you pack, think about the order you're going to be putting your kit in your bag. I've found a way that works for me, which is thought-through, but you should experiment and discover what is best for you.

### Main compartment

- The first two items I put into the main compartment are my sleeping bag and Gore-Tex bivvy bag, which are already inside a sealed, waterproof "canoe bag" or dry bag. Where I sleep is sacred to me, and I will do whatever I can to keep that dry. Once they're inside, they will start to give your bag some form, which will make packing the rest a little easier.

- Next to go in is my hydration pack, which is filled with three litres of fresh water, which I'll slide into the main compartment, and then feed the tube so I can easily access it when walking.

- I then pack my tarpaulin and hammock, putting them together in another dry bag. If you're out in the wild for more than one night, and it rains the first evening, you'll need to separate the tarp and hammock to keep the wet tarp away from the hammock, and this is where the dry bag comes in handy.

- The next layer inside the main compartment is a woollen jumper and any additional items of clothing I think I might need.

- Finally, there is a waterproof bag containing a map and compass (though I might have that out with me).

## Side pouches

- Cooking kit.

- Personal hygiene kit and towel.

- A metal tin that has been on many adventures with me, crammed with yummy food. That's likely to get quite messy so I would keep that inside a waterproof bag, though a carrier bag would be fine.

- Gas-burner inside a stuff sack.

- A water bottle and a crusader cup. My set-up changes depending on the seasons, but I take up to four litres of water with me. While that's going to add up to four kilograms of weight, it's likely you will need plenty of water on your adventures. Make sure your water bottle is in a pouch that's easy to access; think about which side would be easiest for you to reach.

- Thermals in a waterproof bag.

- Foot care kit in a waterproof bag, including fresh socks.

## Top flap

The things you need the most should be the most accessible.

- First-aid kit.

- Whistle.

- Two torches – a head torch and a regular torch with a red filter (deer and other animals can't see the red light so won't be disturbed, but be mindful that this does not allow you to see contour lines on a map).

- Cold weather hat, some gloves and a snood or neck covering.

- Spoon.

- Spare batteries for torches.

- Two gas lighters.

- New, unused emergency life straw.

- Insect repellent.

- Millbank Bag for water filtration (see page 85).

- Sewing kit – splitting your trousers in winter on a micro adventure is less than ideal.

- Spare shoelace – as well as its obvious use, it comes in handy to tie and secure a multitude of things.

As a Marine, I would think carefully about where I put my roll mat as I always wanted to be breaking up my profile and making it harder for the enemy to spot me. But that's obviously not a consideration now, and I attach the mat on the back or sometimes on the base. You might prefer putting it on top – it's up to you.

You might also want your whistle attached to the outside of your bag for easy access. You never know, that could save your life. Many modern day sacks have a whistle built into the chest strap buckle.

## STAYING CLEAN IN NATURE

Keeping clean in the wild was essential in the Marines. It's not an exaggeration to say that cleanliness helped you survive – you needed a comb as well as a weapon. From the Arctic to the jungle to the desert, we were trained to deal with a variety of environments, and wherever we were, hygiene was crucial.

Knowing how to wash was a key part of our basic training. As recruits, we had to re-learn everything we thought we knew about washing. The drill instructor got in the shower in front of about 60 of us, and showed us how to clean ourselves, even demonstrating how to wash your private parts. When I was training or on operations, I sometimes went two weeks without a shower or the luxury of warm water, which is where wet wipes came in handy.

Maintaining your personal hygiene is important for anyone who is going to be in nature for a night or more. If you're able to wash, clean your teeth and even comb your hair when you're out in the wild, you're going to feel better about yourself and are much more likely to have a positive experience.

If you can come back clean from a camping trip – and by that I mean just as clean as when you walked out the door – it shows you're able to look after yourself in the outdoors.

From the moment you step into the wild, your body is going to be producing more oils than it would have done if you had stayed home. That's your body trying to waterproof itself. Those oils are essential for protecting us from the elements.

You'll probably also be sweating more – you're almost certainly moving and exerting yourself more than you would do day-to-day. Carrying a large bag on your back and walking maybe 20 kilometres before setting up camp, will build up sweat and grime; dealing with that, and finding a way of keeping clean, is of paramount importance in the wild.

# Wild toiletries

For those who are happy to forage for their toiletries, there are some natural ways to keep clean.

## Teeth

- Should you forget your toothpaste, you can always use charcoal (though obviously it needs to be cold as putting hot charcoal in your mouth isn't the best idea). Charcoal attracts impurities and works reasonably well, so why not give it a go, but it's also quite abrasive and is something I would only suggest using for a day or so.

- Chewing a couple of mint leaves, which can be quite easy to find thanks to their pungent smell, will help to keep your breath fresh.

- You could make a cup of mint tea and swill your mouth with it. And you can tip any cold mint tea leftovers over yourself as the volatile oils will help to clean your skin.

## Washing

- You might choose to make a wild soap by digging up some red campion plants, crushing up the roots and boiling them, to release their saponins.

- Conkers also contain natural saponins which can be extracted by splitting them in half and steeping them in hot water.

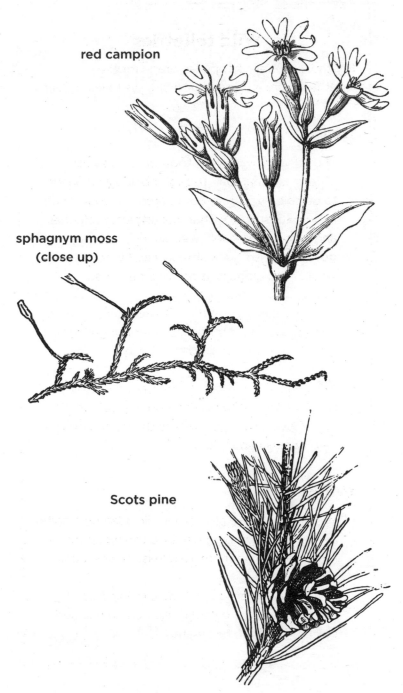

red campion

sphagnym moss
(close up)

Scots pine

- If you need a sponge, try to find some sphagnum moss, which contains trace amounts of iodine, which is used by doctors to treat wounds.

- You can wash yourself using Scots pine needles, which have anti-bacterial qualities. You can recognise the Scots pine thanks to the light orange hue of its bark and how when you pull at the needles they come away in twos. A rhyme to remember: "needles in two with an orange hue".

  Collect some needles, crush them and add to hot water. Let it cool a little before washing in it – it's great for any cuts or abrasions you've got too.

## Salve

- If you have sore or irritated skin, consider washing using the inner bark from a willow tree as that contains salicylic acid which soothes and heals.

- Meadowsweet is also great for you both internally and externally. Used to effectively treat a wide range of ailments from stomach upsets to eczema.

- Some people like pine tar soap, but this is going to make you smell of fire (which is fine by me as I love the smell).

## What to carry

The problem with using soap when out in the wild is that it will be wet and slimy after use, which you don't really want in your bag. That's why I tend to take a liquid or gel soap, always going for the eco option, along with some anti-bacterial hand gel. If you're going somewhere with mosquitoes or insects that bite, take some tea tree wipes, which will repel them. There are small lightweight options for brushing your teeth, like the mini brushes and toothpaste tubes that you will often find in hotel bathrooms.

Besides toiletries, and a sealable bag to keep them in, you'll need a container or two for your washing routine. You could bring metal containers or, a favourite of mine, a foldable, textile "10-litre kitchen sink", which I have used all over the world.

A decent towel is a must. I've got a microfibre towel which is big enough to go round me, so if I ever want to I can hopscotch across the forest floor with a little modesty. If you're looking to pack light, you could go for a smaller towel, but I don't think you'll ever regret taking a larger one.

## HOW TO WILD WASH

You'll need around a litre of water to have a good wash. Heat up most of that water on your fire or burner, and then add the remaining cold water, as you want it to be warm rather than hot. Ideally, you should end up with water that's around 40 degrees Celsius, which is about the same as your shower at home. Warm water won't just be more comfortable for you; it will also help the skin to breathe and allow you to clean yourself properly. Once you're happy with the temperature, soak a cloth in the water and then add some soap and work up a lather.

Stripping off isn't necessary to wash yourself in the wild, and is definitely not recommended in the winter – something you learn as a young Royal Marine recruit on a bitterly cold morning in Dartmoor. In cold weather, you should wash while keeping all your clothes on and expose as little skin as possible to the air.

As you're going to be washing everything with the same cloth, the order is important. You don't want to find yourself cleaning your bum and then needing to wipe your face. Here's my recommended order:

1.  Start with your face.

2.  Move the cloth down the front of your top to clean your chest.

3.  Put your hand up your top to scrub your armpits, which should be a priority area, as if you don't keep them clean you can quickly develop sores.

4.  To wash your back, put your hand inside your jumper, and wash from top to bottom.

5.  Give your thighs a good wipe by putting your hand down the top of your trousers.

6.  Roll up your trousers to the knees, or as high as they will go, to scrub your lower legs.

7.  Repeat steps 1–6 to rinse.

8.  Repeat with towel to dry. (When it's cold, you might want to rinse and dry each part of your body in turn, rather than drying everywhere at the end.)

9.  Finally, wash the parts you must always leave until the very end, your bum and private parts, which you can clean by putting your hand and cloth down the top of your trousers.

10. Rinse and dry.

I'll also clean my feet every evening just before getting into my sleeping bag, as part of my night-time routine. One thing I learnt from my time as a Marine was the importance of looking after your feet, and that's why I always pack **zinc oxide tape**. If you have any hot spots – where it's red and angry and it feels as though you might be about to get some blisters – applying some zinc oxide tape will help soothe your sore, tired and aching feet. Another essential, I've found, is **athlete's foot powder**. You might want to put some powder in your new socks so you're good to go in the morning.

When you've finished washing, don't pour the dirty water into a stream or river or near any water source, even if you have been using an eco-friendly soap. Make sure you're a good distance from any running water before tipping your waste water on the ground.

And how about the washcloth? Give that a good spin to get the worst of the grime and water off it, and then wring it out as best as you can and leave it to dry overnight. You want the cloth to be dry before putting it back in your bag but you should find it dries reasonably quickly, especially if you already have a fire going and you can hang it close to the heat.

While I recommend collecting water from the river or stream, I don't want to be encouraging people to wash there. Even with eco soaps and the best of intentions, you're introducing volatile chemicals and compounds into a water source which is naturally balanced. All sorts of animals rely on that water, and, you never know, another human might be trying to collect water downstream.

As young Commandos, we were taught to have a foldaway comb with us in the field. That wasn't about trying to look smart, but about checking your hair and scalp for ticks or cuts. By combing your head every day, you will quickly find out if you have a tick or if you have cut your scalp without realising.

A comb is very light and will fit easily into your bag. I also wouldn't leave home without at least one pack of tissues, as they will prove very useful. You'll use them for cleaning your face, drying yourself and also for your toilet routine. What were you planning on wiping your bum with? In the absence of toilet paper, my go-to choice would be the hazel leaf. It has thousands of soft, tiny, fine hairs and is ideally suited for wiping grubby mouths and ... bums. You will need to use several leaves at once (I suggest a minimum four at a time) to avoid a disastrous toilet experience!

## COFFEE AND CHORUS

If you organise yourself the night before, with your gas-burner and fire-striker or lighter within reach, it's possible to make your morning cup of coffee without leaving your hammock or tarp and exposing yourself to the cold morning air. You can make your drink and enjoy it while still being fully cocooned. What's great about that moment is the realisation that you don't have to be anywhere. You can sip your drink while enjoying a slow start to the day, maybe while looking at a map and planning the next bit of your adventure, or while doing nothing at all but listening to the dawn chorus and appreciating your surroundings.

In the summer, the dawn chorus can start as early as 4am, when day breaks. It quite often starts with the smaller birds, with their chirping getting louder and louder. About an hour in, and you'll notice the low warbling of the pigeons. The smaller birds will then start to speak up as if they want to drown out the pigeons. They're almost saying, "Shush. We're the best singers around here." Next are the harsher sounds of crows, ravens and magpies. Inside all of us, when we hear that sound, is a natural urge to want to get up and start the day. But don't feel as though you have to. Do what you wish, and always at your own pace.

Whatever you do in the morning, don't just whip open your sleeping bag and let the cold air rush in. The best approach is to incrementally put your clothes back on, layer by layer, and enjoy the treat of your toasty, fresh pair of socks, before getting up. If it's particularly cold, also put gloves and a hat on, as well as a coat, before getting out.

Once dressed and out of your cosy space, consider a second hot drink. As well as tasting great and giving you a caffeine hit to get you going, it will help you stay warm out there in the wild.

## REVERSE ORDER

When breaking down camp, do everything in the reverse order to when you set it up. The very last thing you should be doing is taking down your tarpaulin, shaking it off, scrunching it up and putting it in your bag. Then, if it starts to rain as you're breaking your camp down, you can just ride it out underneath the tarpaulin.

## DON'T LEAVE A TRACE

Look around you carefully to ensure you have picked up everything you brought into the wild. Leave no trace, disappear and carry on.

Not leaving rubbish behind in the outdoors is about personal pride and being part of a team effort. We all have to share the great outdoors. As time goes on, and our cities grow, there's going to be less and less to share, so it's ever more important that we look after nature. You should be leaving footprints and nothing else.

If you're going to be enjoying the outdoors, you need to take responsibility. I quite often find campfires that haven't been tidied away, with small balls of foil. That foil gets everywhere and animals will end up chewing on it. I've heard of farmers doing post-mortems on animals and finding foil and plastic inside their stomachs.

And if you're camping on the coast, then rubbish and plastic could easily blow into the sea or ocean and harm marine life. We should all do our utmost to leave no trace.

## REWILDING REMINDER

- It's only when you spend a night sleeping under the stars that you get to know who you really are.

- You might think you know yourself, but can you be sure how you will handle the challenges of being in the wild and whether you can rough it for a night or two away from the comforts of your home?

- Sleeping outside is the chance to learn some new skills, but also to discover so much about yourself.

- All being well, you'll realise you're capable of so much more than you imagined.

# 7

# FORAGING

If I'm hungry tonight, I can simply open the fridge and cupboards to find something, or even just reach for my phone and order dinner on an app. I don't forage through necessity – I forage because there's something very special about going into the outdoors and sourcing wild food. Foraging gives me a warm feeling of self-reliance, and that's something I'll never get from ordering a takeaway.

When you go out foraging along the hedgerows or in the forest, you'll be sourcing the freshest food you will eat all week, as it's never been anywhere near any supermarket plastic packaging. If you know what you're looking for – and I'm going to introduce you to a few of my favourites in this chapter – foraging can promote healthy eating, boosting your gut health and immune system.

As a Marine, I didn't know much about foraging, and my diet wasn't anything like as diverse or as healthy as it is now. Back then, the highest priority with my nutrition was getting "op massive" – putting on muscle before going on operations – which I did by consuming tubs and tubs of protein powder. I wasn't thinking enough about looking after myself for the long term, such as enhancing my gut health. But that's all changed now.

Today, I can identify the plants I come across outdoors, and even know what you can eat and what you can't, how they taste and what they will do for you. When I look at nature now, I don't just see a sea of green, but all the individual elements: the edibles, the medicines, the poisons. If you have that skill – and also know what each plant or tree has done for us historically – that's the crux of ethnobotany. It's not just about doing what you must to survive but working in harmony with your natural environment to enhance your quality of life. And that skill will put you head and shoulders above others in the outdoors.

On days when I go into the outdoors to forage, I attach a pouch to my belt and line it with a zip-lock bag that will help to keep everything fresh. Other days I might be in the outdoors for another reason and I'll just spot something tasty. As I walk, I'm constantly looking around, scanning the woodlands and hedgerows for what's on offer.

I'll forage all year round. I collect apples, blackberries and cherries. I make cider, jams, chutneys, and all sorts of other concoctions. One year, I foraged enough damsons to make six bottles of wine, which I seem to remember went down pretty well with the family at Christmas. There's a rosemary bush near my house and if I'm passing I'll sometimes take a couple of clippings for my Sunday roast.

# GOOD FOR YOU

I feel as though I now have a greater appreciation of the plants that are growing in the wild and how they can help to improve my diet and overall health.

## Good for your gut

Foraged food will inevitably improve your nutrition. For better gut health, we should all be eating around 30 different plants a week, which might sound a lot but is achievable. And research has shown that good gut health correlates to good mental health. I've read up on how Professor Tim Spector from King's College in London has shown how there's a link between your diet, your brain and mental health.

Our diet today isn't what it once was, with so many foods processed and stacked with sugar, but if you can eat something straight from a hedgerow, you're consuming it in its purest form. It hasn't been messed about with and that brings massive benefits; that's closer to what we're designed to eat.

While I still eat meat, I don't have it every day, treasuring it as a hunter-gatherer would have done. I've greatly reduced what I buy from the butcher or supermarket, preferring to fill my chest freezer with whatever I shoot with my rifle. I have a fair amount of wood pigeon, as pigeon breasts are absolutely delicious. If I've done some pest control with a shotgun, I'll eat grey squirrels too, though usually only the legs as it can be hard work getting to the rest of the meat.

## Good for your wallet

You can't say this about much in the modern world, but foraging is free; you can get delicious, nutritious food without having to reach for your wallet. Some of my earliest foraging experiences were with my grandfather when I was just a small boy. He would take me for walks in the summer holidays, and we would collect sweet chestnuts from my primary school playing fields. We would take them home and roast or mash them. That was my introduction to the chestnut and its sweet, lovely flavour; it's also full of carbs and starches, making it a great survival food. He was a brilliant grandfather, and made foraging fun for me. We would also play "golf" with conkers, whacking them with his walking canes to see who could propel them furthest across the fields.

## Good for your heart and mind

Foraging is a great excuse for getting outside, exploring what's in your area and doing some exercise – as you'll often have to walk for a while to get a decent bunch of plants (it's not like strolling the supermarket aisles, where everything you want is within easy reach).

Above all, foraging is incredible for your mental wellbeing. I always feel better after a morning's foraging for the ingredients for my wild spring salad or for the wild garlic immune booster. It's the quiet confidence of knowing that, if something disastrous happened to supermarkets' supply chains, I can still find food for my family. If I need to be, I can be self-reliant.

# SAFE FORAGING

In all the years I've been foraging, I've never poisoned myself, thanks to the knowledge I've acquired from ethnobotanical courses, speaking to professional foragers and herbalists, and from teaching myself through reading and getting out into the wild. I can be confident that the wild chips and wild salad I'm having for my lunch won't do me any harm.

You do need to be able to identify the plants you're looking for and how to tell them apart from lookalike plants, which can sometimes be poisonous. I like to use all my senses to identity plants – even when I'm very certain I know what I have foraged. So I will smell the plant to see if there's a distinctive aroma that might confirm my thinking. If you're not sure, you can always consult Google to check that you're foraging the right plant.

You might wonder why I have bothered to learn the Latin names for plants, and also why anyone is still using a "dead language" for these living things. Well, it's to avoid any confusion. The same plant often has more than one "common" name in English, depending on where you are in Britain, or around the world. To be sure you're foraging the right plant, you need to know the Latin as that never changes.

A piece of advice on dog wee. If you find a patch of plant you want to forage, don't pick anything right on the edge of the path, particularly if people walk their dogs there, as it's likely their pets have cocked a leg on the leaf you're thinking about eating. Urine from other animals, such as foxes and badgers, may also be present all over the countryside. Washing your harvest before cooking or eating is essential.

# THE FOUR FS

Always keep the four Fs in mind when foraging.

- Foliage

- Fruit

- Flowers

- Fungi

These are the four types of food you can take from the countryside, so long as you have the landowner's permission. You must also do so sustainably. That means only taking what you think you're going to need, rather than being greedy and harvesting as much as you can carry.

To aid sustainability, I will rotate where I forage, as I don't want to keep on hammering the same piece of land again and again.

You cannot forage for commercial gain. I'm not going to go out and pick 25 kilograms of mushrooms from the forest and sell them to restaurants; but I know this is happening all around Britain, and I find that sad. People don't understand that the mushrooms have a key role in the ecology of that forest; if you take huge amounts of them you're going to be upsetting the natural balance.

# RAMSONS:
## YOUR FREE IMMUNE-BOOSTER

You can buy all sorts of products to boost your gut health and immune system, but they're not cheap. So, why not create your own amazing free product which you can add to a wide range of dishes? It's made from ramsons, a type of wild garlic that grows in Britain, and is very simple to do. It involves a process called lacto-fermentation, which cultivates the good bacteria, lactobacillus, that we need in our gut. This bacteria will help us to have a more efficient digestive system, which gives us a stronger immune system. It is the same bacteria you find in sauerkraut and kimchi, and I think we would all benefit from eating more of it. A healthy gut gives you a healthy body and a healthy mind.

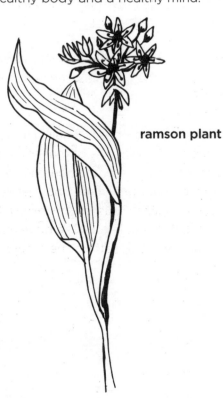

**ramson plant**

When foraging for ramsons, look for its flat-bladed, soft leaf accompanied by little white flowers. It's often found in damp and shaded areas, such as by a river or on the edge of a pond. You'll know it's nearby as you'll smell the garlic.

Another way of checking you've found the right plant is to rub its leaf. When rubbed, the ramson leaf will become translucent and give off a garlicky aroma. Select plants with no impurities on the leaves.

## Ingredients

- Ramson leaves and flowers

- Sea salt

## Method

- At camp or home, rinse the leaves with cold water, and check no other plants, such as ivy, have crept in among them.

- Sterilise a jar, including the lid, with boiling water; you don't want any bacteria in there apart from the ones you're trying to cultivate.

- Put the washed wild garlic in a bowl, and add some sea salt. Salt will kill off the unhealthy bacteria, leaving only the bacteria you want.

- Pound the garlic with a stick. This is going to

take a while so don't be in a rush. What you're looking to do is to break up all the cells inside the leaves, which will release the water inside. You'll notice a chemical process start to happen as the liquid turns green and bubbles away.

- Keep pounding until the pulp is smooth.

- Tightly pack the jar with the garlic and salt pulp and ensure it's covered with the residual liquid.

- Pop the lid on, which should form a tight seal.

- Leave the jar in a dark cupboard for at least a few days to ferment.

As it ferments, the sugars turn to lactic acid, which is a natural preservative. The longer you leave it in there, the more the bacteria will continue to multiply and the product will get better and better, though there's a trade-off at some point between bacteria and taste.

## How to use

You can enjoy that rich garlic flavour with a wide range of food, but it's something you *add* to a meal rather than the main event. It goes very well with pasta dishes, but whatever you're adding it to be careful not to heat it up too much as the heat will kill off the good bacteria. Also avoid putting it with sugary foods, as that will reverse the fermentation process and encourage the growth of bad bacteria in your gut.

# WINTER SYRUP

Another great immune booster is a legendary winter syrup that you often hear older generations speak of (and I can understand why they rate this).

## Ingredients

The quantities in this recipe are pretty relaxed. It's not a problem if you have more of one sort of berry, or like a slightly less sweet syrup.

To make a medium-sized jar, try a handful of each of the below.

- **Elderberries** contain tannins that have anti-inflammatory and anti-bacterial properties, among other health benefits

- **Hawthorn** berries are a source of cardiac glycosides that help to strengthen your heart

- **Dog rose hips** have thirty times more Vitamin C than an orange

- **Honey** contains antihistamines and helps to soothe your throat. Use a good dollup of honey to ensure the berry juice becomes sticky and syrupy.

## Method

- Sterilise a jar, including the lid, with boiling water; you don't want any bacteria in there apart from the ones you're trying to cultivate.

- Remove the pips from the hawthorn berries and mash the berries.

- Remove the seeds from the rose hips by cutting them in half with a knife and taking out all the seeds one by one (this can be a little painstaking).

- Put the elderberries, hawthorn berries and rose hips in a saucepan on a medium heat. Add the honey and stir regularly until you have a thick, black liquid.

- Place the syrup in a jar and store in a dark cupboard.

## How to use

Take one spoonful of syrup every morning throughout the winter months.

# BURDOCK ROOT: WILD CHIPS

Going back to pre-historic times, the burdock would have been used as a key part of our diet as the root is high in starches and sugars. It has since been eclipsed by the potato but harvesting the burdock, and making chips in a pan on the campfire, is still a great thing to do with the family. The burdock root can take some digging, so be prepared to burn off some calories before you get to enjoy your wild chips. Over the years, the burdock has been used to treat a variety of ailments and conditions, from rheumatism to infections. Its sweet and nutty flavour makes an excellent chip.

Burdock is easily identified by the leaves that took a bit like rhubarb, and by the roots that look similar to parsnips, though often slimmer and longer. Nevertheless, it's worth confirming you have the right plant by holding it to your nose to see if it has a nutty smell. That smell carries through to the taste. It's a bit like a sweet potato, or like carrot, potato and nut all in one.

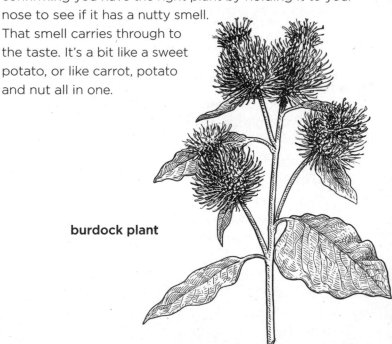

**burdock plant**

When you find one burdock plant, you tend to find lots. And it grows in abundance and all year round in certain parts of Britain, so you can sustainably forage them.

## Ingredients

- Burdock root

- Cooking oil

## Method

- It's only the root that you want, so dig up the plant and remove the rest. While it's safe to eat the leaves, they are very bitter and don't taste good.

- Take the roots back to your camp or home, and wash well to remove the earth.

- Peel off the outer layer to uncover the creamy white interiors, which is where the sugars are.

- Chop the root down the middle and cut into chip-size pieces.

- Put some oil into a pan and shallow-fry the chips for between five and ten minutes until they start to go golden brown. If your fire is hot, and the roots are young and tender, it will be closer to five minutes.

# WILD SALAD

Spring is the best time of year to go out foraging for wild salad leaves. The hedgerows are teeming with wild edibles.

## Suggested ingredients

- Wild primrose leaves and flowers (don't confuse this with foxglove, which is poisonous)

- Wild garlic

- Hairy bittercress

- Young hawthorn leaves (not a particularly exciting flavour, but a good healthy green)

- Cuckoo flower, also known as lady smock (spicy, peppery and mustardy, and often used to finish off fancy cuisine; it will add some bite and zing to your wild salad)

- White-dead nettle (has a distinctive square stem and doesn't sting)

- Young hogweed shoots (also good fried in a little butter). Beware of picking giant hogweed – which looks the same but far larger with a thick, hairy and mottled purple stem – as this is poisonous.

## Method

Wash your gathered leaves in water and pat dry.

**REWILDING REMINDER**

- When you forage, you are working with your natural environment to promote the quality of your life; you're eating more healthily while also enhancing your gut health and your immune system.

- Just as importantly, foraging is brilliant for your mental wellbeing, as you're demonstrating that you're self-reliant and can provide for yourself and your family.

- Foraging means getting outside and exploring your local area, which is always going to do wonders for how you feel.

# 8

# CARVING & CREATING

I didn't learn to sharpen or care for knives as a Marine. I had a different relationship with knives when I was in the military. We were working at such a relentless pace on operations that it was easier to hand back our trashed equipment, draw fresh items from the store and then go again. I would destroy knives breaking into ammunition boxes and dull the tips by prodding the ground to find the exact location of IEDs or landmines, as was the practice back then after hearing the dreaded double solid tone from the metal detector. Or, when operating somewhere more tropical, I would give my big jungle knife to the armourer and he would put an edge on it ready for when I went out the next day.

It's only since leaving the Marines that I've picked up how to care for knives, and that's required study and practice. If you invest time in learning to look after your knife and your axe, then they'll look after you in the outdoors.

They say you're only ever as sharp in the wild as the tools you're carrying, so if you have a dull blade, and you're not planning on doing anything about it, or simply don't know how, you're going to be restricting how much you can do in the wild. Discover how therapeutic it can be to take care of a knife. I've heard of people getting very creative with their knife care – including using a Land Rover window edge to refresh a blade or turning a ceramic mug upside down and using that edge. Here, I'm going to introduce you to *my* tried-and-tested methods, with gold, silver and bronze options.

## CHOOSING YOUR KNIFE

Before I get into maintenance, let me help you choose a knife for your adventures. This will be your primary tool and will be used for many different tasks. I use my knife every day. It's a humble piece of kit, but an essential one. I would advise against taking a kitchen knife into the wild, as it is likely to snap and stick in your hand the first time you use it. Only carry a knife that has been specifically designed for the outdoors, and is therefore more robust than something you might use for chopping onions.

I care so deeply about the knife I use that I designed my own. I turned my dream knife into a reality through a very long (several years) process that involved drawings, research and design phases and then a number of prototypes. With all the knives I had bought in the past, I had immediately seen what their shortcomings were and where the manufacturers had cut corners with materials or design. Companies have approached me in the past to promote their knives, but I could spot their shortcomings so didn't sell out and put my name to an inferior product that I didn't believe in, and which would have inevitably let me down. Collaborating with a knife designer who shares my values and ethics, and who is himself a veteran, I set out to create the perfect bushcraft knife – and I think we achieved that. The quality is exceptional, with its Niolox steel and carefully considered details; we didn't once compromise on quality.

While I have gone on to sell a small number of these knives, making money was never the goal. All I cared about was creating a beautiful, handmade knife I could use every day. While I love how it looks and how it sits in my hand, the most important consideration is how it performs. After all, a knife is a tool.

People used to say that you can't get stainless steel blades as sharp as carbon blades, but the technology has moved on so I wouldn't pay much attention to that chatter. It's up to you how your knife looks, but its looks shouldn't affect how it does its job in the outdoors.

When shopping for a knife, consider the following:

- **Cost**. The knife we created is expensive, costing hundreds of pounds, but don't feel as though you have to spend anything like that much. You can get something pretty decent for a reasonable price. As your skillset increases, by all means go out and buy a more expensive knife if you wish.

- **Accessories**. Some people like to have a sheath for their knife, and these come with or without fancy bits attached, such as a sharpening stone and a fire-striker.

- **Blade width**. You might have seen heavy-duty survival knives on the market that are 4, 5 or even 6 millimetres wide, but I don't think you need anything as chunky as that. The knife I designed is 3.5 millimetres across, which I think is the optimal width. Unless you're using the knife incorrectly, you're not going to break a knife of that thickness.

- **Bevel type**. I would choose a Scandi grind over a hollow or convex grind as you will find that easier to sharpen. A Scandi grind is capable of hard work as well as fine carving and food preparation, such as skinning an animal. I would also encourage you to select a blade that starts very early from when the handle stops. The first inch coming out of the handle is the belly of the blade, and that's going to give you the most power and control.

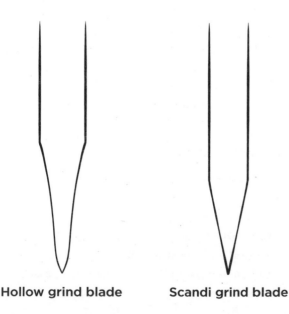

**Hollow grind blade**    **Scandi grind blade**

- **Grip**. Look for a knife with a good quality grip, as that's going to give you the control you need when fine carving or working in wet weather – the last thing you want is for it to slip out of your hand.

# SAFE USE OF A KNIFE

You're not in the circus, so don't ever throw your knife across the forest. And only in an absolute emergency would you think about tying it to the end of a stick and using it as a spear. When using and handling a knife you need to be smart and responsible. I can't stress enough the importance of using a blade safely.

## Where to do knifework

Never use a knife between your legs, as you only have to slip once and you could slice through an artery. If you're right-handed, you should be doing your knife work over the right hand side of your body and working away from yourself. If you're left-handed, you should be using your knife to your left. Remember, if you were to cut yourself badly while somewhere remote, you would need to react very quickly – administering first aid within minutes – and it would be hard for help to reach you.

## How to handle a knife

Ninety per cent of your knife work in the outdoors will be done with the belly of the blade, because that's the part that will give you the greatest power and control. As you move up the blade, away from the handle and towards the tip or point, you have to apply more force to get the same result. When using the belly of the blade, you would usually have all your fingers on the handle.

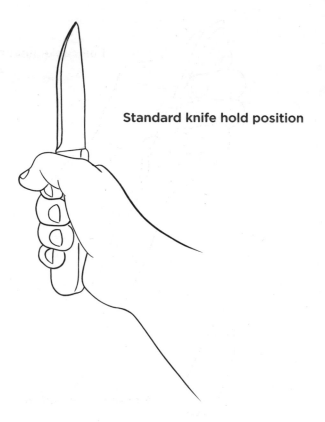

**Standard knife hold position**

For more advanced knifework, when you're going to be using the curved part, you can hold the knife in the **half-choke position**, with your thumb on the side of the blade, for extra control.

If you're doing even more delicate work – such as carving off small bits to finish a wooden spoon – you could **fully choke** the blade by holding it between your forefinger and thumb, right up on the curved part. Lay your fingers and palm below. Your palm may be on part of the handle and your other fingers will almost certainly be lying flat to the rest of the blade. That will give you greater control when carving, such as when scalloping to make the neck of a spoon.

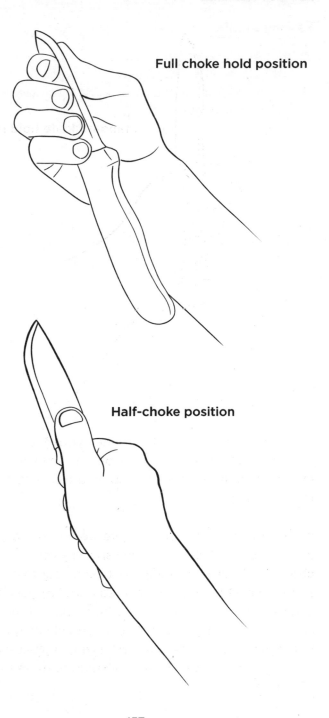

**Full choke hold position**

**Half-choke position**

## Passing a knife

When passing someone else a knife, try presenting it with the pommel at the base of the handle first, with the blade uppermost. It may sound a little silly, but I've used the phrase "pommel to person and it's all going belly up" to teach people ("belly up" is reference to the belly of the blade).

A tip is not to secure the knife with your finger rested across the blade. Maintain eye contact with the person you're handing the knife to and talk to each other, with some verbal acknowledgement when you're making the exchange.

Of course, the safest approach is to put a knife in a sheath before handing it over, but that's not always so easy when you're camping as the sheath might be attached to your belt.

# KNIVES AND THE LAW

I would encourage you to check the law – even local bylaws – about using a knife or an axe. It's unlikely to happen, but you don't want to take the risk of running into any legal difficulties when travelling by train or bus or walking around the city before going into the wild. If you're carrying a knife in the United Kingdom, the blade has to be three inches or shorter and non-lockable. You can't be walking into your local supermarket with a 12-inch blade hidden inside your trouser leg. But it is deemed okay to have a knife on you that's longer than three inches if that's appropriate for its use, such as doing some kind of activity in the outdoors.

Being responsible means being discreet. If I'm travelling on a train with my bushcraft knife, for example, I will keep that in the leather sheath at the bottom of my bag and certainly not clipped to my belt and on show for the world to see or potentially access.

# LOOKING AFTER A KNIFE

Your knife isn't a samurai sword. While you want to have a sharp edge, you can take that too far and risk chipping and damaging the steel. A safe way to test the blade is to try it on a piece of paper – you should be able to easily slice through it with little force.

Between uses, coat your knife with a little oil to protect it. If you don't have any oil with you in the wild, you can use your own natural oils – put the tip of your finger into the crease beside your nose and wipe the oils you find there on the blade.

When you need to sharpen your blade you have what I call gold, silver and bronze options.

## Gold – Japanese wet stones

These stones – which I think of as my gold standard – need to be soaked in water for a good ten minutes before use. Made from aluminium oxide, these stones have numbers on them indicating how coarse and rough they are – the lower the number, the coarser it is. My stones are 600, 1500 and 3000, and I wouldn't ever suggest going any higher for bushcraft.

Before deciding which stone to start with, weigh up how worn, used or damaged your knife is. If you've been working your knife particularly hard, you're going to select a coarser, rougher stone to begin with. Work the knife on that stone before switching to another stone that's not so abrasive. Continue using different stones – gradually moving to a higher number, so less coarse – until you're happy that the blade is sharp enough. If the blade is very blunt to begin with, you'll need to use several stones. Do this regularly and you might only need to use one stone.

A colouring pen is a must when learning this skill. Before I get to work on the stones, I colour in the bevel, which is the part of the blade from the cutting edge up to what's known as the shoulder, which is where it turns back into a regular piece of sheet steel. The beauty of using a pen is that it will show me where I have and haven't been with the stone. If I'm doing this correctly, the ink will disappear with each stroke, revealing the shiny metal beneath.

## How to sharpen

Lay the blade on the stone, which has a rubber base, keeping it in position on a flat surface. Place two fingers on the guard of the handle (the bit nearest the blade) and two on the blade and tilt the knife slightly so that the cutting edge makes perfect contact with the stone.

As smoothly and as methodically as you can, with only the weight of your hands bearing down, push the knife away from you and all the way up the stone, doing around eight strokes. Now do a few more as you move up the blade, but this time with more of a sweeping motion at the end, with the two fingers on the blade finishing at the diagonally opposite corner. That allows you to make perfect contact all along the edge, which is curved towards the end.

As you work, keep checking the ink is coming off, and use your thumb to check an edge is coming back, gently dragging it across, but never along, the blade. If you can detect the edge riding over the bumps and contours of your thumbprint, then it is sharp. Next flip the blade over and start at the far end of the stone, pulling it back towards you. With your thumb on top, you're in complete control, ensuring you're making good contact.

Once you have reapplied some ink with the pen, repeat the process with the next stone. Don't be afraid to re-wet the stones from time to time, sprinkling on some water with your hand.

## Silver – Small dry stone

When you're out on the trail, you won't want to lug around your set of Japanese wet stones, but you can rejuvenate your knife with a smaller dry stone which you can keep inside a pocket on the sheath. I always carry a dry stone, which is my silver option, as that ensures my knife is always at its best.

One advantage is that it doesn't require water. One side is made from aluminium oxide and will remove metal and put a new edge on your knife while the other side, which is ceramic, is for honing. While the stone doesn't come with a rubber base, I like to lay it on top of my phone as that has a rubber case, giving me some grip and stability as I work. The one I carry is four inches long, which is significantly smaller than the Japanese wet stones, which makes sharpening your knife a little trickier, requiring smaller movements. But after you've done this a few times, you'll get a feel for what works and what doesn't, and you'll be able to sharpen the entire blade from the belly to the tip in one stroke.

161

Once you're happy with the new edge you have created with the aluminium oxide side, turn the stone over and use the smoother ceramic side to complete the task.

## Stropping

Stropping your knife with a piece of old leather glued to a piece of wood. Lay the bevel of the blade on the bottom of the leather and drag it up towards you, and then back down again. Do that 50 times. You're not really removing any material from the blade but on a molecular level you're standing up the edge of the blade. But you probably don't want to carry one of those around with you in the wild. This is where it helps to have a good quality leather belt - and not a fake leather one – as you can take it off, put it around a fallen tree or log and ensure it's super taut. Again, you're stropping up and down.

You might want to carry a small pot or tube of stropping paste, which you rub on to the belt, and which helps to polish and tidy the blade. With a dry stone, a real leather belt and some stropping paste, I can maintain my edge when I'm in the field.

## Bronze – No-nonsense wonder tool

As a Marine, I would sometimes use the Lansky Blade Medic tool – which is small, lightweight and requires little to no skill – when in transit. I didn't need somewhere stable to work, but could use this in a moving vehicle. I would run a blade through the V shape, which is made from tungsten or ceramic, and it would put an edge back on fast. I consider this my bronze option as it is extremely aggressive on your blade, removing a lot of material and potentially damaging it. If I used this tool regularly my knives would disappear to nothing. It's so aggressive that

I wouldn't ever use it on a high-quality blade. However, it's fine to use occasionally on your less expensive knives, and there's also a ceramic part and another surface for finishing it off. This is a great option for someone who doesn't have the time, or the knowledge or skill, to look after their knife.

Another tip for looking after your knife. If you're going to be using your sharp blade again and again to split some firewood, I would suggest making yourself a hardwood wedge and using that instead, in combination with a wooden mallet.

# Making spoons

Making spoons has been one of the constants in my life over the last few years. I started doing it during my first few days in the recovery centre and it's not uncommon now for there to be wood shavings covering the floor of my house.

While you can carve spoons anywhere, I feel as though there's nowhere better than round a campfire. Even more so if you're doing it with others. Often a group can be sitting there in comfortable silence making spoons – everyone fully focused on their own personal creations, yet with a strong sense of togetherness. You don't need to be talking to be reconnecting.

Making spoons is meditative for our over-stimulated brains. I can happily sit and carve a spoon for four hours as my brain won't be thinking about anything but removing that next bit of material. I don't go down a rabbit hole, rather I'm in the moment, in the present, with the piece of work I'm making. They say that busy hands make for a quiet mind, and I undoubtedly feel relaxed making a spoon, putting my energy into something creative. The only thing you have to be conscious of is to always cut away from yourself to avoid injury.

Every spoon I've made tells a story. Each one is functional, but also emotional. Your spoons will make for great presents for friends and family, as they will be able to tell how much care and attention have gone into them. Over time, you will learn about the different wood types and what their natural limitations might be in terms of the design. If you're keen to embrace your creative side, maybe start with a feather-stick and then move on to a spoon. If you discover you enjoy doing this, maybe progress to carving a lovely Swedish wooden cup, known as a *kuksa*, or even a fruit bowl.

**a simple wooden spoon**

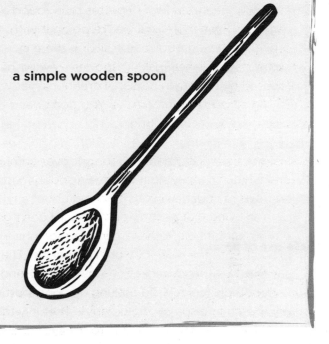

# AXES

## Choosing an axe

In Britain, you don't need a big axe; you can get the speed and force to bust open firewood with a smallish axe that fits inside a rucksack. An axe is one of the essential items you'll need for bushcraft, and there are hundreds to choose from. So, which one is right for you? Much depends on what you're going to be doing with it, but the bottom line is that you need the head to be heavy enough to break open wood. It should also allow you to cut down small diameter trees if required. Secondary uses are wood carving and occasionally knocking pegs into the ground.

They say firewood heats you four times: when you fell it, when you split it, when you stack it and finally when you burn it. A full day of splitting firewood is back-breaking; if you're going to be doing a lot of that, you want a decent axe you can rely on.

## Safe use of an axe

Before getting to work with your axe, check there's no one behind or in front of you as they could be hit if the head breaks free and goes flying through the air. There's also a danger that the axe could come out of your hands, which could be lethal.

If you're swinging a small axe – such as one you can fit in your pack – I would advocate always being down on one knee. If you're standing and you miss the wood, or the blade glances off, you could hit yourself in the leg. Using an axe requires concentration and both hands. If you feel as though you need more accuracy, push your hands up

166

the handle so it's closer to the head; the trade-off here is some loss some of power.

If you're using a full-size axe, place the head on whatever you're trying to split, such as a log, and have the handle touching your belt or belly button. From that position, take half a step back. If you're right-handed, your left hand will be on the lower part of the handle and your right hand will go right under the head. As you bring the axe up, keep the head and weight of the axe close to your body. You're taking the shortest way up and the longest way down. As you bring the axe down, don't focus on the head but what you're trying to hit. As you swing, your right hand will slide down the shaft until it joins the left hand. The weight and speed of the axe head should split the wood open, sending the pieces flying.

If you're going to be splitting timber for a while, you might end up with a sore back. To protect yourself against that, instead of repeatedly bending over to pick up the split timber pieces, I use the end of the axe head, known as the toe, and dip it in the freshly split-open face of the wood in line with the grain, which will clasp the metal toe and allow me to lift the timber into my arms.

## Looking after an axe

As with a knife, you want your axe to be sharp but not too sharp. If it's too sharp that could cause you problems when busting open wood and any other heavy-duty tasks. If you make your edge so sharp that you can almost shave with it, there's a risk that it will chip or break. So, there's a balance to be found when sharpening the head with a fine file. When sharpening a knife, you're moving around the stone, but with an axe you're holding the head in one position while driving the file down on either side of the blade. A couple of strokes will help to bring the edge up and deal with any small chips or dings. Next I'll turn to the stone I keep inside my knife sheath, doing circular motions on the blade.

To protect the head against rust, apply some oil with a cloth, taking care to cover all the metal. Spread and rub that all over the head. When you're not using your axe, protect the head by covering it with a leather sheath. But that sheath also deserves to be looked after, and every now and then I'll brush in some shoe polish.

When you're splitting wood, or maybe bashing a tent peg into the ground, you will sometimes glance off slightly and that can cause chipping and other damage to the top of the handle, where it meets the head. If you've got any boots that have come to the end of their lives, pinch the laces from them. Wrap those laces round the top of the handle near the head, forming a spongey and protective layer that's going to absorb some of the energy from any glancing blows.

In the Marines, we used a lot of amalgamating tape, which is stretchy, rubbery and offers excellent grip. If we were going to be boarding the enemy's boats, we would put that tape on the handles of our assault rifles and other weapons. I now use that material – which you should be able to get from your electrical store – on my axe. I'll wind that around the laces, maybe doing a double or triple layer, for maximum protection. If you can't get hold of amalgamating tape, you could use fabric tape or zinc oxide tape, which is also fabric-based.

The wooden handle also needs some love and attention: apply a light coating of oil with a cloth.

# FOLDING SAW

One other tool I should mention – and which you might come to rely on in the wild – is the folding saw. It's light, easy and effective to use. With relative ease, I can go through decent size timber pretty cleanly. There are lots out there on the market to choose from. You can find folding saws made from soft and forgiving steel, with retro-fitted hardened teeth, which is ideal for beginners. Something like this might be very useful if you're looking to cut wood to put on a fire, and it doesn't cost very much.

**REWILDING REMINDER**

- Taking care of your knives and axes can be extremely therapeutic.

- You're putting an edge back on (and we're only ever as sharp as the tools we use), but it's so much more than that – it's the feeling that you have given yourself the best possible tools to thrive in nature.

# PART THREE

## RECONNECT

Sitting around a campfire, you instantly feel an enormous sense of wellbeing. Your eyes will immediately fixate on the flickering, dancing flames. You don't want to look away. Almost as quickly, your mind will slow and calm down, and you will feel safe.

That comes from thousands of years of understanding, passed from human to human, that with a fire you have the ability to cook, to make water safe to drink, to provide light and warmth, to ward off predators and to signal for help.

Fire also creates the atmosphere that allows you to have real conversations, to perhaps talk more openly and deeply than you would anywhere else.

If you have mental health issues or you feel overwhelmed by what's happening in your life, Part Three is for you, but it will also help all readers.

I'm going to show you how to lay fires, and even set you the ultimate bushcraft challenge of starting fire by friction.

I'll also give you some guidance on how to have better conversations around the flames. Seated around a fire, you'll find that you can more easily reconnect with others, and also with yourself.

# 9

# RECONNECTING AROUND A FIRE

When I was at my absolute lowest point, when I was numb from top to toe, the only place that felt right was the woodland. And the only thing that gave me any purpose and strength was making and sitting around a campfire. Gathering twigs and logs, feeding those into the fire and staring into the flames ensured my mind stayed in the here and now, rather than replaying trauma and spiralling somewhere darker. It was also a fire that kept me alive that winter night when I wanted to switch myself off and ended up passing out in the woods after drinking most of a bottle of rum. Without the heat of the fire next to me, which continued to flicker and smoulder while I slept, I could have frozen to death.

From the gorgeous smells to the gentle crackling sounds it produces, to the mesmerising visuals of the dancing flames, I adore everything a campfire brings. Lighting a fire is often the first thing I do on arriving at my woodland camp. Once the fire is lit, I feel as though the camp is open and that my time in the woodland can really start. It's a simple thing, but fire brings a feeling of safety and security, but you must also respect its power. Fire has had me transfixed for years, long before it saved me. My love for fire goes back to when I was a boy, but even as a teenager that love never tipped over into getting a thrill from torching stuff just to watch it burn – I'm not that kind of fire-worshipper. What I adore about fire is how it makes me feel and what it does for me, including letting me have real, honest conversations that I might not have anywhere else.

My life lessons in lighting, maintaining and sitting around fires have mostly come as a civilian. In more than ten years in the Marines, I only ever remember sitting and talking around a campfire once, when we were given permission the night before a training exercise in brutally cold conditions in northern England. As a Commando, most of your movement is done at night, under the cover of darkness. On operations, you're in a non-permissive environment, which is to say that others don't want you there and you shouldn't do anything that might alert them to your presence. You're being super-tactical, and a campfire is highly non-tactical. The only other occasion I lit a fire in the field as a Marine was on a five-day survival exercise on Dartmoor during basic training, but it was a small, discreet fire as I had to ensure it didn't give my position away.

## FIRE – AN ESSENTIAL ELEMENT

Fire gives you so much, including light and warmth. It also provides a sense of home and comfort. It's reassuring to know, sitting in the great outdoors, that you have the ability to provide for yourself. Cooking food on a fire has been done for hundreds of thousands of years; and that's how many people all over the world who don't have the luxury of an oven to cook their food today. For them, the lighting of a fire every day is imperative. On an adventure in Lesotho, I met young shepherd boys, who start work from as young as five, and who need to be able to start a fire to be able to do their jobs on the mountain.

Fire also allows us to heat water for washing ourselves, to purify drinking water and to sterilise tools (even if that's just to sterilise the end of a needle to pop a blister). Lighting a fire means you can extract vitamins and organic compounds from plant matter (otherwise known as making a cup of tea). Fire can be used for preserving foods and tanning hides. While it's okay to burn organic waste to keep your camp tidy, DO NOT incinerate plastic and other rubbish.

I've seen first-hand how people use fire to signal if they're in distress or danger. On patrols in Afghanistan, I would watch the locals tracking our progress by burning car tyres and lighting other small fires. To keep the enemy guessing where we would go next, we had to keep changing directions as we moved across the landscape. In so many ways, fire can save your life. In certain parts of the world today, fire wards off apex predators – if you're going to be sleeping in open bits of Africa, lighting a fire could be the difference between you being eaten by lions or not. If you get into difficulty in the wild, a fire can also be a signal for help, allowing you to be found.

## FIND MEANING IN FIRE

Vikings believed that the gods would send them messages in the fire, and today our brains are always looking for meanings in everyday things. Next time you're sat around a fire, see if you can see shapes or figures in the flames. Some people say they can spot skulls, horses or other wild beasts.

If you're dealing with anxiety, you may well think you see something representing those concerns in the flames. The flames move so quickly that you'll often see a glimpse of something. Take from that what you will. If I spot an image of something I don't want to see, I tell myself it's OK as it's in the flames and gone in an instant; I cast it into the fire so I no longer have to carry it with me.

## THE ALTERNATIVE POWER OF FIRE

Since leaving the Marines and going on this journey in the outdoors to manage my complex Post Traumatic Stress Disorder, my appreciation for fire has only grown. I've come to realise that, on top of everything else, a fire lets you do something extraordinary: connect with others on a meaningful level. Talking around a campfire is something that humans have done since the dawn of time. If you put people around a campfire, you're going to have real conversations – they're going to be honest, possibly raw. What those conversations won't ever be – and I can assure you of this – is superficial. We send emojis or hide behind text messages or emails, but when someone is sat there with you around a campfire – staring you right in the eyes sometimes, with the fire the only form of illumination – you have a real conversation. Sitting around a fire you will start to rediscover the lost art of conversation.

I'm also confident that those conversations will bring about learning and self-discovery much faster than burying yourself in your phone and scrolling through other people's social media feeds about how amazing their lives supposedly are; that will often only make you feel worse. The campfire, meanwhile, cleanses your soul and mind: sitting around it with others will help you feel better.

Humans are tribal. I like to think of sitting around a fire sharing stories as an ancient art – an art that will help many of us to reconnect with others and also, most importantly, with ourselves. A campfire is a forum where you can air any issues you have. More often than not, you will find a way of addressing the problems in your life, and come away from the fire with a fresh perspective on life.

Your tribe is often your family first and foremost, though I understand that isn't always the case, as families can be poisonous environments for some. Sitting around a campfire is a wonderful way to reconnect with your family, especially with the oldest generations. For hundreds of thousands of years, from civilisation to civilisation, we humans have been listening to our elders and learning from their wisdom. But in modern society I feel as though we ignore those who have gone before us because we think we know better, and the result is that we make mistakes that we otherwise could have swerved. So, invite your family to come together around a campfire and get talking – you'll soon be strengthening and reconnecting those family bonds.

If you put two strangers next to a fire, they're going to get to know each other very quickly. I see that every day on the courses I run in my woods, and it's lovely to witness. You'll feel great if you can take the chance, when around the fire, to help someone solve a problem in their life.

A fire transcends everything and is a great leveller. It doesn't matter what your story or background is, once you're all gathered around a fire everyone feels connected. It's a team effort to keep a fire going in the wild, everyone has to pull together. Fire creates responsibility – you all have to feed the fire to keep it alive and so have shared control of it.

And because fire can be very destructive, there's a responsibility not to misuse its power. Spending time around a fire brings people together in a way that's unparalleled. The reality is that – unless you really know what you're doing – people don't always fare so well on their own in the wild. To get the most out of being wild, you need to work with others, as part of a tribe.

Sitting around a campfire, underneath an old parachute for protection, and there's nowhere I would rather be. And if you add in eating together around the fire, your sense of tribe will be even more enhanced.

## USE THE POWER OF FIRE WHEREVER YOU ARE

Campfires don't have to happen only in the wild – you could create a similar effect in your garden with a fire pit, or even by simply lighting a candle and placing it in the middle of a table, as restaurants do. But if you have the opportunity to be somewhere a little wilder you are likely to create an even better connection with others.

Out in nature, you're away from the hustle of the modern world, so you already have some distance from what's bothering you in your life. There's also nothing else around to focus on. There's something so calming about sitting there and staring into the fire, which I think of as humanity's oldest television. Looking at a fire, something wild gets reignited inside every human – you can't take your eyes off the flames. Sometimes you stare for so long, you zone out. If that happens, go with it, and don't try to pull yourself out of that state as your brain obviously needs the break.

# HOW TO HAVE REAL CONVERSATIONS AROUND A FIRE

I didn't ever open up as a Marine. There simply wasn't any real downtime or space in that role for unwinding. I served during a highly industrious period for the Marines – we saw a lot of action – and I never found a chance to open up and to unload my mental burden. We all needed egos to operate at a level that kept us alive. When eight of us were going out on a night patrol into enemy-held territory, with an unknown number of enemy fighters out there in the darkness, we had to believe in our own hype, just as a champion boxer would before getting into the ring for a fight. However, having such big egos was also deeply unhelpful for creating an environment in which you could speak freely and without judgement. In that culture, self-awareness was perceived as a weakness.

It was only after buying some woodland, and sitting and talking around campfires, that I found a safe space where I could have real conversations. My first tip – and this is a fundamental one – is to select a space where you'll feel completely at ease.

## No judgement

There are no real rules for talking around a campfire, but, as with any situation, it's helpful not to be judgemental of others and what's going on in their lives. Understand that you have bias – we all do – but find a way of parking it, as only then can you give someone the best of yourself and really listen. That means listening to their choice of words and the larger message behind what they're actually saying. And relax in the knowledge that the others are doing the same.

## Go with the flow

When you take your seat by the fire, you might well have an idea of a conversation, even a difficult conversation, you want to have. But you might also find that some of the best conversations happen when you don't have an agenda, when you approach the fire willing to talk about anything, to let your mind wander and go wherever it needs to. The realness will come out. When you're not trying to project into a phone, to show the world a curated or edited version of yourself, a more honest and real version of yourself will appear. In a world with so much superficiality, most people are searching for real conversation. Around a fire, everyone gets the real you – the good, the bad and the ugly – and you get the real them.

## Share experiences

When I'm sharing a fire with someone who has experienced hardcore trauma, it can help if I tell them I've also gone through some gritty stuff as well. I'm not trying to compete with their stories – I just want them to understand that they're sitting with someone who has also been there and has an understanding of how it feels. But you also don't want to set someone off with your stories, or to imprint fresh details in their minds, so there's a judgement call to be made. I'll pick bits of my experiences that I think people will relate to. It's a judgement call about when and how much to share.

There's often a fine line to tread, but the more time you spend talking around a campfire, the more you will come to know when to speak and when to stay silent.

## Be supportive

My message to people who have been through trauma, or who are feeling low or worthless, is that they can turn it around. Talking about it around a campfire could be the start of their road to better mental health and wellbeing, and to finding a way of managing whatever it is that they're going through. Let the other person know this is an opportunity to open up, that you're here to listen and help them in any way you can.

This support doesn't just come through words; around the fire you will be reading other people's non-verbal communication and they will be doing the same to you – looking at how you sit, stand and move. For many people, the fire will be somewhere to direct their attention to rather than having to make eye contact with you, which may make it easier for them to have a tricky conversation. Others may use the responsibility of feeding the fire as a way of keeping their hands busy, which in turn allows them to talk freely and openly.

## Listen and be aware

If someone is in full flow, you should respect that and not butt in. You have two ears and one mouth for a reason. However, there are some rare occasions where that flow could be detrimental to them and they might not even realise it – the unloading process could be causing them enormous distress. If you pick up on that, you can perhaps stem that flow by interjecting or asking a question, just to try to nudge them off that thought pattern. But, by and large, I wouldn't disturb someone when they're soul-searching and unburdening themselves around a campfire.

## To drink or not to drink?

Some people find that if you drink alcohol your conversations can go even deeper. Adding alcohol into the mix can help some people relax and open up conversations; but ultimately alcohol is a depressant, so be aware that it could also act as a catalyst for something unsettling or upsetting. Often a clear, coherent brain solves a problem better, especially when there are other clear, coherent brains around.

# FIRE MAKING

Even if you go into the outdoors intending to only use a gas-burner, having some idea of how to start a fire is important as you never know when it could come in handy. There might even be a situation in which being able to make a fire saves your life. I covered the process of making a basic fire on pages 88–89 in the chapter on making a wild cup of tea. However, I will expand on a few important features of the process here.

## Consider location

Considering where is appropriate to light a fire is extremely important. You might be in a semi-ancient woodland, which is carpeted with bluebells that have taken 400 years to establish themselves. The last thing you want to be doing here is leaving a big fire scar. As much as I love fire, there are certain situations where I realise that I don't actually need one and that it would be better to do all my cooking and boiling water on a gas burner. Certainly, never light a fire next to a river. You may have this idyllic vision of a fire by the river, but all it does is cause considerable fire damage on the riverbank. Vegetation near a river should be flourishing, but instead it's often flattened, crushed and burnt. Remember that others – animals and humans – are also using the wild – it's not all about you and what you want to do when you're in the outdoors.

## Prep properly

Fire-lighting can be trickier than you think, which is why you should always carry a back-up ignition source.

Before you go to light it, make sure you have prepared the fire properly, and have all the raw materials you need (see pages 87–89). Before it was ever a dating app, tinder is the light, soft and easily combustible material that gets the initial flame going.

You'll also require kindling, which are slightly thicker pieces of wood. Your tinder could be natural or man-made – all year round, I collect natural fibres and plant matter for tinder. This includes the tops of water-thistle heads, which at the end of the year can burst into a fine grey highly flammable fluff that's easy to collect.

Another great winter tinder is the dried and almost translucent seed pods of a purple flowering plant called honesty, which can be easily picked and contain oils that make them highly volatile. Other options are the stems or stalks of water thistle, dry grass, the common nettle, a woodland shrub called herb bennet, and bunches of twigs that are dry enough to easily snap in two.

If you can find any burnt pieces of wood from a previous fire, they are always useful as they take less energy to get going as the process of carbon release is already in mid flow. Depending on the time of year, I sometimes take cotton wool with me to get the initial flame going.

As you gather everything you need, remember to keep it off the forest floor to prevent it from getting moist.

## Feather-sticks

Let me introduce you, if you're not already familiar with it, to the natural fire-starter, the two-in-one product you can make yourself that will give you both tinder and kindling while also promoting mindfulness in the wild – the humble feather-stick.

A feather-stick is a straight piece of wood with beautiful curls on one end that increase the surface area, and you can make it yourself with a good whittling knife.

There's a whole world of stuff out there for starting fires, but feather-sticks are ideal. You light the end with the curls, and when that gets going the other end will start to take; you then lay some thicker pieces of wood on top. You want a dense bundle of feather-sticks to effectively catch a flame; a technique I use is to snap the feather-sticks in two and fold them back on themselves.

From a mental health perspective, making feather-sticks gives you far more than the potential to start a fire. You can lose yourself while making them, which is why it's often the first activity I ask people to do when they come on my courses in the woods.

# How to make feather-sticks

- Find straight pieces of wood that aren't too knotty or chewy, and which will fall open easily when split with an axe.

- Split the wood, then use your knife to turn thicker bits into thin pieces.

- Once you have your thin, straight pieces, use the belly of the knife blade (the part closest to the handle) to create fine curls.

- For safety, remember to always work away from yourself.

Make sure the curls overlap so that the feather-stick catches light and the fire spreads evenly

One of the hardest things to learn is being able to stop making the curl before you get to the end of the piece of wood, and not push off the beautiful curl you've just made. If you already have five or six curls and then push the next one too far, they all fall off – which is extremely frustrating. There is a technique to prevent that. If you're right-handed, hold your knife across the front of your left knee, pulling it in tight so the spine is in the soft part of the knee. Your right hand is just there to support the knife. You can then do the more delicate work by using your left hand to pull the wood through and across the bevel of the blade, twisting or tilting the knife to pick up the edge. If you're left-handed, follow the same method, but swap the hands and knees.

People really get into making feather-sticks. I watch them go through all sorts of emotions during the process. Initially, they may bully all the curls off the end and get cross – to the point where they may have to walk away and have a cup of tea to compose themselves. However, by the third or fourth stick, they'll be using the knee technique, creating fine curls, and will love it.

Although the aim is to make something to burn, many people treasure their first few feather-sticks so much they take them home with them.

# DIFFERENT TYPES OF FIRE LAY

On page 89 we covered the basic criss-cross fire lay to enable you to quickly make a cup of wild tea. Here we'll go into a bit more detail on other fire lay patterns, as the type of fire you create often depends on whether it's day or night, whether you want to slow it down or if there's a storm coming.

## STAR FIRE

The most basic fire lay, the criss-cross fire, burns through your fuel very quickly. If you wish to slow your fire down, you can easily turn that into the far more fuel-efficient star fire. This is a fire lay I use often as I think it gives you more bang for your buck. A star fire is easier to control than a criss-cross fire. One challenge, though, is that you'll have to harvest larger pieces of wood, for which you might need an axe or a saw (see page 166).

### Method
- Create a platform, as for the criss-cross fire. This is important as you'll need the elevation – by raising the ends of the wood slightly in the middle, the energy is kept centrally.

- Make the criss-cross fire lay, but instead of criss-crossing the large pieces of firewood, feed in six pieces of large diameter wood, to create a star shape.

- The pieces of wood should be sitting on top of a mound of ash, burning gently. Every so often, push the pieces of wood closer into the fire to feed the flames.

This is the type of fire, sometimes known as a hunter's fire, that native Americans used to create; everyone would have responsibility for one corner of the fire, and for feeding in a piece of wood. Other cultures have also embraced this type of fire. If everyone is feeding in a piece of wood, and looking after their part of the fire, that really promotes the sense of tribe.

If other campsite duties take you all away from the fire, you can safely leave it smouldering rather than burning by pulling the six pieces of wood away from the centre of the fire. On your return, you can push them into the centre again, giving your fire life again by blowing on it. Form a diamond shape with your two index fingers and thumbs and put that against your lips to create a 'straw' which you can blow air through. Even if you think the fire has gone out, please don't stick your head too close to it when blowing oxygen into the base to give it a bit of a push.

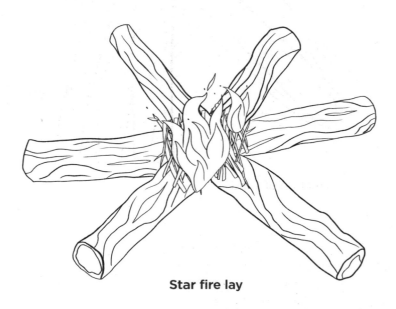

**Star fire lay**

## V FIRE

This is the only type of fire that I've seen survive a serious storm, when giant trees were coming down all around us in a forest.

If the wind is whipping through your camp, it will push everything off a criss-cross or star fire, breaking it up and extinguishing the flame. If your fire goes out, and your wood is soaked through with rain, it's going to be very hard to start again.

**V fire lay**

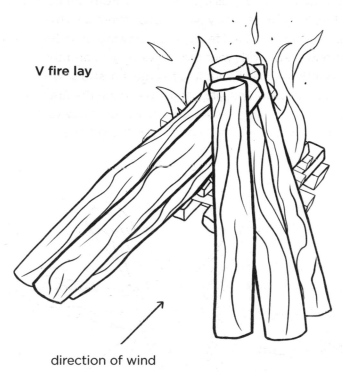

direction of wind

**Method**

- As soon as it looks as though a storm is on the way, start turning your fire into a V shape, moving the logs so the point of the V is facing into the wind.

- Keep on piling up the logs or pieces of wood until the fire is big enough to last for as long as you need it to. You're funnelling the wind into the fire, constantly feeding oxygen to the flames (though in extremely windy conditions, you may wish to protect your fire slightly at the front).

- The V fire is self-feeding, which is a fascination of many people, and makes life a bit easier. As each piece of timber burns through, the one on top falls down and into the flames. If the fire has been built correctly, it should self-feed all the way down to the last piece of timber, and keep your fire alive throughout.

- To keep off the rain, you could cover the larger logs with smaller diameter pieces of wood.

- When the storm has passed, you can change your fire back to a star fire if you wish.

## LONG LOG FIRE

This is the type of fire I choose to sleep next to, as it provides a wall of fire from head to toe. The long log fire has saved many lives. I once spent four days in the wild in winter, without a sleeping bag or tap water, as I wanted to practice my survival skills. With the temperature dropping to minus four at night, creating a long log fire was vital to stop me freezing and allow me to get some sleep. Ideally, the fire should be a little longer than you, as that ensures you're getting warmth all along your body. I'm just under six feet tall, so I'll build a fire that's seven feet long, using long branches and large diameter pieces of wood. I use slightly smaller pieces of wood for my star fire during the day and the larger pieces for my log fire.

**Method**

- You're looking for small diameter trees – ideally dead hard wood – and need to put the thicker stuff on the edge. You're probably going to need an axe or saw to prepare the wood for this fire (see page 166). The smaller, more combustible wood should go in the middle to help rev it up, as you want to build up that ember base.

- You can turn a star fire into a long fire. Take the logs that are arranged in a star formation and lie them end to end so they're about half a foot from each other. Drag some of the embers from the centre to the left and right as that's going to help the fire to burn. (Should you wish to, you can reverse this process in the morning, putting the logs back into a star formation and returning the embers into the middle.)

- If there's a slight slope, sleep on the raised side to get the most benefit from the fire, since heat rises (it also reduces the risk of a burning log rolling towards you). Sleep one and a half steps from the fire – that seems to be the ideal distance as you will get maximum heat without being in danger.

- Another consideration for where to build your long log fire is wind direction, as you don't want to be getting a face full of smoke when you're trying to sleep. I choose to set up my camp so it's side on into the wind, but with the wind coming from slightly in front of me. You definitely don't want the wind coming from behind you, going over the top of your shelter, hitting the smoke which will then eddy back in your face.

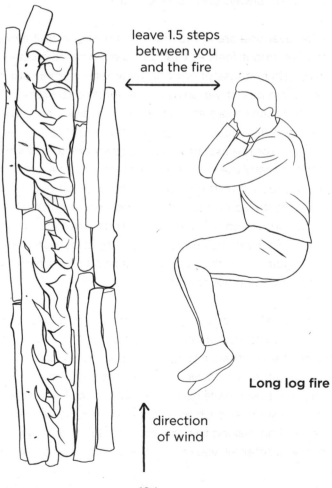

leave 1.5 steps
between you
and the fire

**Long log fire**

direction
of wind

# FIRE BY FRICTION

One of the most challenging (and also most rewarding if you succeed) tasks you can set yourself in the outdoors is making fire by friction. I tried and failed many times as a boy. As an adult, I was shown the correct method on a bushcraft course and I finally had some success – I still remember the feeling of achievement that washed over me. However, I'm not always so fortunate. Even though I've now been teaching fire by friction to others for years, I can't always get this to come off; so don't be surprised if you don't always end up with a fire.

Wherever you are in the world, it's tricky to make fire by friction, and it feels as though it's even more challenging in Britain because of our damp climate. It's unpredictable. There are lots of variables in the fire by friction process, which means there are all sorts of ways it can go wrong. It's often described as a survival technique, but after trying it for the first time, you might want to ask yourself if that's really the case. Racing against the setting sun, maybe feeling a little weary and cold, you'll experience many of the same frustrations and challenges that your ancestors would have done. The difference is that our ancestors' lives would often have depended on getting a fire going, and they would have had to persevere until they saw the glow of an ember.

If you feel like a challenge and want to get a greater sense of how our ancestors lived, give it a try. If you do manage to start a fire, that shows you have a strong understanding of the natural world. However, do not rely on this method; and don't ever leave home without one or two other ignition sources, such as a lighter. As your life doesn't depend on making this fire, you should try to enjoy the process. After all, you're in the wild to have a good time.

I'm going to introduce you to the bow drill method, as it has the mechanical advantage of using a bow to turn the spindle, which is a great help in our unpredictable climate.

## Fire by friction set

The first step in the bow drill method is to make your own fire by friction set, which comprises:

- Spindle/drill

- Hearth board

- Bearing block

- Bow

- Catch tray/ember pan

The aim is to make a powder that will drop on to the catch tray, and the powder will go on to become the glowing ember once it gets hot enough.

The spindle should be roughly a foot long, cylindrical and about three quarters of an inch in diameter. One end is sharpened to a point like a pencil and will be held in place by the bearing block. The point should have minimal surface area so it spins freely. The other end of the spindle is dulled, shaped like the bottom of a wok, and will sit in a divot on the hearth board. You need a greater surface area as that will give you maximum resistance for more fiction and heat. Select a thinner piece of wood for the bow (about as thick as your thumb), which you complete with a piece of string.

You can make your set from a giant log, but that will involve a fair bit of carpentry and time. It's easier to go into the forest and hunt for pieces of wood that are close in size and shape to what you require, as then you won't have to do as much knifework. But you do need to know which woods and shapes you're looking for, how to create the tools and how to problem-solve.

You need wood that's dead and dry, but not so far gone that it's too soft – if you can make an indent on the wood with your nail, it's too soft. The wood also needs to be bone-dry. I've found that the best way to test for moisture is to put pieces of wood against my lips. If it feels moist, it's not going to be any use. While finding the right pieces can take some time, that very process gives you a chance to explore the woodland. And remember you won't have to do this every time you make fire by friction: once you have your set, you can use it again and again. Don't worry too much about the catch tray/ember pan, as you can just make that from a wood off-cut.

## The Bow-drill method

As I've already emphasised, preparation is key for any fire. When making a fire by friction it's even more important that you have everything ready. The last thing you want is to have a glowing ember but no platform, tinder or kindling. You'll need a source of tinder and kindling that's good to go for when you make your spark. In this scenario, I suggest you use a bundle of dry grass for your tinder.

If you're right-handed, hold the bow in that hand. Lean on your left knee, with your left foot pinning the hearth board to the ground, while your right leg ought to be behind you and tucked out of the way. While that position will feel a bit odd at first, it will allow you to swing the bow freely. Bring your left hand, which is holding the top of

## Friction by fire set-up and elements

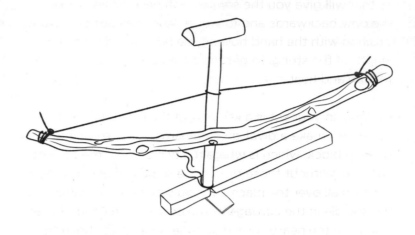

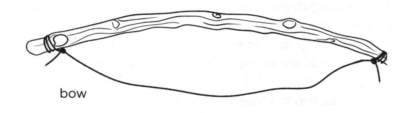

bow

spindle/drill      bearing block      tinder

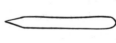

catch tray/
ember pan

hearth board

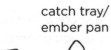

the bearing block, round to the front of your knee. If you can, try to lock your wrist off round the front of the shin, as that will give you the stability you need as you drive the bow backwards and forwards. Adopt a neutral wrist position with the hand holding the bow, and use the full length of the string, to get maximum speed and therefore friction and heat.

Bedding in your set is a key part of the process. Using my knife, I make a divot on the hearth board and on the bearing block, which is where the two ends of the spindle will turn. Without those divots, the spindle is going to be jumping all over the place and you won't get fire. Wrap the spindle in the cordage of the bow, put one end of the spindle in the hearth board and the other in the bearing block, and see if it wants to turn. Be aware that you're always going to get a few initial problems. Turn it gently to begin with and always be prepared, with your knife at the ready, to do some more carpentry to ensure the spindle's ends are sitting where they need to be. Make any adjustments, and then go again. You will be creating a bowl shape in the hearth board.

If the powder is going to drop into the catch tray below, you need to cut out a small slice of the bowl shape. Take your time doing this as you need to get this right. If you make that too big, you won't have enough surface area in the bowl to create the friction to reach those high temperatures. But if it's too small, the powder won't drop through.

You'll almost certainly find that you need to do more carpentry as you go through the process. Perhaps the end of the spindle and the bowl shape in the hearth board are becoming too smooth. In effect, they're polishing each other, when what you want is for them to be rubbing against each other and creating friction. If that's the case, scrape the knife across the end of the spindle a couple of times, which should roughen it up. Another common problem is that the sharper end of the spindle can become worn down and needs to be sharpened with a knife.

If you hear some screeching, you have moisture on your set, which means you will not make fire, no matter how good your technique is. You have to keep working, creating enough friction and heat to get rid of that moisture, before you have any chance of making a fire. You might want to do all this on a stump to keep everything off the wet forest floor.

You will be burning through a lot of calories, and probably getting a tired shoulder. But just imagine if your life depended on creating an ember – you would definitely find a way of getting it to work.

When you get the first puff of smoke, that's an encouraging sign that the set and the method are working and that everything's heating up. But you'll still only have generated heat of around 200 degrees Celsius, and you're going to have to achieve around 700 or 800 hundred degrees to create the ember you need. The moment you see smoke, increase the intensity, working the bow twice as fast as you were before and also pushing down twice as hard with the bearing block. Doing that for ten seconds or so will give you the best chance of creating a decent ember that will drop into the catch tray below.

Once the precious ember has been formed, pick up the catch tray. The ember should start to glow like the end of a cigarette. Tip the ember inside the tinder bundle, and gently blow into it, steadily and upwards. If you blow too hard, sparks will start to jump about inside the bundle, which you don't want. Look at what the wind is doing and position yourself so you're working *with* nature and not against it. When the smoke changes to a straw colour you know the bundle is about to burst into flames. When it does, lay the bundle on to the platform you have created, adding your other tinder and then kindling as it gets going.

Congratulations! You've achieved something that most people wouldn't even attempt.

# RESPECT FIRE

Respecting the power of a fire means safety is paramount. Movement around a fire should be concise and considered. Never run round a fire, as there's a risk you could trip and land in the flames. For the same reason, don't leave firewood scattered around, as they could be a potential trip hazard; organise the wood into neat piles.

Dress appropriately for your fireside chat. Where possible, avoid wearing clothing made from modern tech fibres which can be extremely flammable. If you've got long hair, tuck that in before going anywhere near the fire as if your hair goes anywhere near the flame there's a risk that – whoosh – you could soon have a dangerous situation on your hands (or on your head).

Ask yourself: do you have the means to quickly put the fire out? At any moment, you should be able to extinguish the flames, so you'll need some water, sand or earth close by.

To keep yourself and your companions safe, don't start a fire on a steep slope, as you don't want burning logs rolling around (this is even more crucial advice if you're planning on sleeping next to a fire).

# PUTTING YOUR FIRE OUT

It's not the done thing to walk away from camp and leave a fire burning. If you're heading off somewhere, always put your fire out. If you walk off and conditions are dry, you could inadvertently start a wildfire, driven by the wind.

Douse your fire with water until it goes out. Start at the edges and keep your head back and out of the way. If you pour water over the centre of the fire, and you're leaning in to see what's going on, there's a chance you'll receive a steam burn, with hot water and debris being spat back in your face. Stabbing the ground with a stick will ensure that the water is penetrating deeper into the soil, and you'll know for sure that your fire has gone out.

When you know the embers are cool enough for you to handle, scoop them up and fling them in every direction, as far and as wide as possible. By the time you're finished, there should be nothing left but a dark mark on the ground.

Before you started your fire, you would have cleared a small area of leaves, mould and other debris until you got to bare earth. Now push all that back over where your fire was. Do that right and you won't leave a trace.

## REWILDING REMINDER

- Sitting around a fire, you'll soon rediscover the lost art of conversation.

- Sharing stories around a campfire, you'll be reconnecting with others and with yourself. Helping someone solve a problem will make you feel good. Or perhaps talking will help you to gain a new perspective on something that has been troubling you.

- Either way, with the warmth of the fire and the camaraderie it induces, you're going to feel better.

# FINAL
# THOUGHTS

As soon as you think you've got everything sussed out,
life can hit you hard. Life is full of surprises, and that's why
I accept I'll forever be learning – about myself and about
the great outdoors.

While I already know a fair bit about nature, there's so
much more – an endless amount, in fact – that I don't yet
fully appreciate or understand, and that's fine. In fact, it's
more than fine, because I'm passionate about furthering
my study of the natural world, and that's why I go to
bed every night with a book. Before I go to sleep, I fill
my head with new information about plants, trees and
the behaviours of wild animals. In the morning, when
I'm back in the wild, I can put what I learned the night
before into practice.

I've always had an inquisitive mind and wanted to
understand more about the world, its people and its
cultures, and that mindset served me well throughout
my travels.

Now, more than ever, I've got this desire to discover and learn about the natural world. The more I know, the more I can enjoy being in the outdoors, and the more complete and human I feel.

## ONE DAY AT A TIME

Life is about adapting. One of the life lessons you acquire from spending time in the outdoors is the importance of problem-solving and picking up new skills to adapt to new surroundings and new situations. And what I have learnt has crossed over into how I manage my complex Post Traumatic Stress Disorder.

If you suffer from PTSD, there will be hard days. I have days when survivor's guilt eats me alive. This leads to self-sabotaging behaviour, as you think you can't possibly deserve the lovely things you have. Some days my paranoia is massive, particularly when I drive into a city. If I'm waiting to pick someone up from the train station, I often can't help but burn myself out by analysing everyone around me to establish whether they're a threat. But the fact I can even step into the station is testament to how far I've come, as that wouldn't have been possible for me a few years ago.

Part of always learning and adapting has been realising that a balloon popping at a children's birthday party can trigger memories of explosions going off all around me in Afghanistan, and finding ways of coping with that.

I still have the occasional dark week when it feels as though I'm "in the hole" – I'm tired and grumpy and might sob my heart out at any moment. But, thanks to rewilding myself, I know I can adapt, learn and move forward.

For the rest of my days, I will be working on myself and investing in myself. It's about trying to create a sustainable battle rhythm for life, whether you're in the wild or in the city.

## LEARN FROM YOUR MISTAKES

If you're going to learn effectively, you need to embrace failure. Nature has taught me that. If you're failing, you're learning – so long as you're willing to accept that you've failed and are prepared to dissect and truly understand where you went wrong and how you can make it work the next time you give it a go.

I'll always remember the time I failed by not paying attention to the type of wood I was collecting for my fire. I had inadvertently gathered lots of soft wood, which burns very quickly, and so at 3am my fire went out and I was abruptly woken by the freezing cold of the winter's night. I had to put my head torch on and go out foraging for firewood. It wasn't a very comfortable experience but I learned from it, and I haven't made that same mistake again.

From burning myself to putting a fire in the wrong place and getting so much smoke in my face that I ended up with red eyes, I've failed plenty of times in nature. But I've always tried to ensure that I learned from where I went wrong.

The first time you try to start a fire, or do anything else suggested in this book, it might not work – but that's no reason to give up. People of all ages are fearful of failure, which means they won't give something a try.

When I talk to people about the purpose and benefits of rewilding, I encourage them to embrace failure, to accept that they're unlikely to get the hang of something first time but to know that they'll get there in the end. I have a quiet confidence, yet know I will fail sometimes. And that's OK, as that just confirms that I'm still learning.

While I may have been passing on some of my expertise in these pages, you and I aren't that dissimilar; we still have so much more to learn about nature and about rewilding. Just thinking about that makes me very happy.

# About the Author

Nick Goldsmith is a former Royal Marine Commando who left the military after developing Complex Post Traumatic Stress Disorder from a busy career in service.

His unique inspirational story of overcoming massive odds through the application of a positive growth mindset has seen him become the CEO of an awardwinning outdoor business, author and public speaker.

Following his military service, he established a distinguished career in the outdoor education and wellbeing sector, founding Hidden Valley Bushcraft in 2015.

In 2016 he set up the Woodland Warrior Programme CIC; a programme of therapeutic activities centred on bushcraft and the natural world, to assist serving and former members of the armed forces and emergency services with the transition into civilian life.

Having served and travelled all over the globe, from the jungles of Belize, the Arctic, to the Australian bush and desert environments of Oman, Africa and Afghanistan, it was a passion for wilderness living skills, coupled with respect for indigenous people and their cultures, that inspired him to use these skills as the vehicle to spread his message today.

Nick is a strong advocate for mental health, having used the outdoors in his own recovery pathway. Through after dinner speaking and appearances on radio and television, he openly shares his story promoting the benefits of the outdoors.

Born and raised in East Sussex, Nick now resides in a rural area of the West Country with his wife Louise and son Finley.

# Further Reading

Here is a list of just a few books that I choose to keep on my bookshelf and whose beautiful pictures and descriptions continue to inspire me to keep learning more and more about my native environment and myself. I will forever be a student of the great outdoors and I am OK with that!

Baker, Nick, *RSPB Nature Tracker's Handbook* (Bloomsbury Natural History, 2015).

Burton, Frances, *Fire: The Spark That Ignited Human Evolution* (University of New Mexico Press, 2019).

Engel, Cindy, *Wild Health: How Animals Keep Themselves Well and What We Can Learn from Them* (Wild Health Body Work, 2021).

Harari, Yuval Noah, *Sapiens* (Vintage, 2015).

Hoffman, David, *Holistic Herbal: A Safe and Practical Guide to Making and Using Herbal Remedies* (Thorsons, 1990).

Jordan, Peter and Kilkenny, Neil, *The Mushroom Picker's Field Guide: An Expert A-Z to Identifying, Picking and Using Wild Mushrooms* (Lorenz Books, 2022).

Phillips, Roger, *Wild Food: A Complete Guide for Foragers* (Macmillan, 2014).

Reader's Digest, *Field Guide to the Butterflies and Other Insects of Britain* (Reader's Digest, 2001).

Reader's Digest, *Field Guide to the Water Life of Britain* (Reader's Digest, 2001).

# Acknowledgements

First and foremost I must give massive thanks to my parents and sister for a rather well-grounded start to this life growing up in rural East Sussex, for putting up with hours of being stood on the sideline of a rugby pitch, subsequently A&E and, of course, generally eating them out of house and home right up until I left home for the Commando Training Centre – the university of life.

A massive continued thank you to Louise for being an incredible wife, business partner, mummy and emotional rock with her constant love and support. For standing by me through thick and thin, through the good, the bad and the downright ugly parts of the recovery process of finding my way back to the light.

To my boy Finley who, since joining us in this world, has taught me much about myself and has changed my view of the world once more for the better.

To those few friends I hold closest: Chris Mitchell, Alex Harle and Karl 'Sledge' St Ledger, whose versions of reality I will entertain, listen to and whose judgement that I trust. Who can get through to me and help me see reason and make sound decisions when experiencing times of adversity or difficulty.

To Selina Cuff, Mark 'Jonah' Jones and Nigel Gifford OBE who have helped me greatly in becoming the professionalised version of myself that today, delivers courses and speaking engagements. Who have had a positive influence on me, giving me a greater level of function both as an individual and in business and who continue to remain in my circle of influence.

To Mark Hodgkinson for his support in making this book a reality and Eliana Holder for her excellent illustrations.